GOOD OLD KIWI IDENTITIES

The Folk who Put the Kiwi into Kiwiana

David McGill

Many thanks for your 'amusing' hospitality.

Love from

Garry e Raewyn

July 2002.

Grantham House
New Zealand

First published 2000

GRANTHAM HOUSE PUBLISHING
6/9 Wilkinson Street
Oriental Bay
Wellington
New Zealand

© David McGill

ISBN 1 86934 077 9

Edited by Lorraine Olphert

Typeset and designed by Bookprint Consultants Limited, Wellington.

Printed by Bookprint International Limited, Hong Kong.

Con

Introduction

This book is a meditation on emerging New Zealand identity. Sort of. It is not a high falutin' academic treatise. *Au contraire*, it is a view from the other end of the spectrum, of a journalist interviewing notable Kiwis about what is making us so. Or, if you like, this is my pick of Kiwi subjects from three decades and three million published words, which is not really excessive given the way hacks are whipped along by their masters. Malcolm Muggeridge confessed to the same number in his dismissive memoirs, *Chronicles of Wasted Time*. You can be the judge of that re this. *Moi*, I enjoyed the ride.

War has generally been seen as the iron forging the soul of national identity, and Gallipoli has been a significant contribution to our character. The Depression of the 1930s was a unifying force, if only in recognising we were all in the same miserable boat. The Second World War was significant for Kiwi camaraderie *in extremis*, for examples of that make-do Kiwi resourcefulness we pride ourselves on, such as patching up and flying RAF rejects with distinction. The war was important for restoring Maori mana, like Gallipoli, at great cost in lives lost. This book has the post-traumatic disorders following war and Depression looming in the pysches of most of my subjects, as they dealt with the less traumatic peacetime development of our identity, much of it to do with our cultural emergence in the broadest sense. For instance, the egalitarian and lone resourcefulness hangover of the make-do, can-do philosophy from our pioneering days in examples as disparate as a helicopter rescue pilot and several cartoonists; in the stubborn, some would say bloody-minded, way three Kiwi conservationists preserved old pharmaceutical items, old cars and an old church; in the way an All Black put conscience before career; in the way a speedway rider quietly encouraged young Kiwis; in the way artists

4

in print, voice and photograph reflected our identity; in the way eccentrics made this a more singular and curiously more unified place.

OE, or Overseas Experience, plays a large part in defining this emergence. Many of those interviewed returned or settled here clearer about wanting to be a Kiwi, and then the struggle began. In many ways this is a book about recognising and respecting our own cultural contribution, the subjects major contributors to the process. Three very different kinds of Maori contributors and three strong political characters played a potent part in the process, the latter involving negative as much as positive lightning rods for the emergence of the Kiwi character. Their opponents and others who confronted the smug Little Britain bureaucratic and cultural establishment have also been significant agents for transformation out of colonial dependency to finding our own voice. Without war, unless you count the neo-civil war of the 1981 Springbok Tour, and without marching down Queen Street to proclaim it, these folk have played a big part in defining and prodding us all into pride in being Kiwis.

I am grateful to Ian Cross at the *Listener* and Mike Robson at the *Evening Post* for giving me such free rein, although the constraints of size and sometimes policies at the time meant I did not use much of what I gathered. This has been rectified here, with my interest in context and feelings and impressions, including those of the interviewer, coming into fuller play. I thank the present editor of the *Listener* and Mike Robson from the get-go for their generosity in allowing use of material from those publications.

Whilst some of my interviews have been updated, they mostly belong to a generation ago, when we were emerging out of a buttoned-down, uptight, authoritarian, middle-aged-male-dominated colonial era. Many of my subjects I chose because they were intent on moving the process along. Thus this collection is aimed at identifying the time when the push was on to be our own little Pacific nation.

To Those Who Put the Kiwi into Kiwiana

'Old Identity': Somebody here before the gold-rushes, a long-term resident, coined by E.B. Cargill in the Otago Provincial Council when he said early settlers should endeavour to preserve their old identity in the midst of all these new chums in town for the 1860s gold-rushes.

The Passing of a
Pugnacious Prime Minister

In mid-1984 I provoked what turned out to be the last interview with Robert David Muldoon, New Zealand's populist Prime Minister for nigh on a decade. Like many before me, not least most of his underlings ... er, Parliamentary colleagues ... I took the lift to the ninth floor of the Beehive with a sense perhaps akin to the last shuffle down death row. I was quaking in my boots or, rather, black slip-ons. Not so my colleague, cartoonist Burton Silver, who had provoked me into provoking the PM with another of his endless well of instant ideas: let's check out the PM's security. Burton wasn't quaking, except with laughter. He had already read Muldoon's palm. But, to start at the beginning ...

At 7.15 on a chill, still and blessedly fine early winter morning we were in position outside the PM's Lower Hutt residence, Vogel House. Specifically, as lookout, Burton and I were lurking outside the service station, with a diagonal view across the road to the Vogel House driveway. Nearby, on red alert in the two other operational motors, were journalistic colleagues Warwick and Geoff and my brother-in-law Sean, the only one with a hair-trigger, rapid-fire, automatic zoom lens state-of-the-art camera. This would prove critical to our success.

Burton and I chewed the thin fat of our declining expectations. The sun was not yet up. It was cold and exposed; the idea was cooling rapidly. I was, after all, the editor of this idea, of the magazine setting it up. I worried over it aloud. Yes, we had checked with two top lawyers and were permitted to photograph the PM in a public place.

But suppose his Diplomatic Squad decided to do a spot check? We had found out through his press office that he did not bother with his bodyguard support vehicles, even though he was advised to.

A police car cruised past. Burton assured me this happened all the time. A few minutes later the car came back, more slowly. Burton didn't say anything. We had been lurking for half an hour, opposite the official residence of the PM, and not just any old PM, not Keith Holyoake, who answered his own door in his dressing gown and talked to complainants and promised to do something. Those days were gone. We were in a much more hyped-up age, for sure, with a very hyped-up PM, who talked loudly *and* wielded a big stick. When Muldoon barked JUMP!, we jumped and jumped, doing the kangaroo conga.

Relax, Burton advised. He has to appear eventually.

Not if he took off out the back way.

There isn't one.

Maybe he left early?

An hour and two more police drive-bys later, I was ready to thankfully throw in the towel. Nothing had happened. No story, but no grief. Even Burton was ready to pack it in. The sun suddenly blazed up into our faces, when with a scrunching of gravel and a blur of acceleration, the smart, metallic-blue first Ford Sierra in the country was shimmying out of the Vogel House drive, across the road and past us. I was half-blind, my eyes watering from the fierce, low sun. I sensed Geoff and Warwick take off, as I stalled the Volvo once, twice, three times. It gave me time to observe Sean on one knee, firing for all he was worth.

Somehow I got going and fell in behind the other two cars tearing after the PM. Warwick was at rally-driving extremes as he careered through the rush-hour traffic and got up ahead of Muldoon, crouched like a dark egg over the wheel. We could see Geoff filming through the back window. Sean was alongside Muldoon, filming. We were coming up behind. We had him in all our sights. It was working.

That is, until Muldoon swerved into the left lane, across it, on to the shoulder of the motorway, accelerated past Warwick and took off along the foreshore beyond Petone. My mouth went dry, drier, driest. I was trembling. Burton was saying something about catching him up. As we did, Muldoon was out of his car talking to a traffic cop, pointing at us! I needed no urging to get the hell out of there.

Back at the office, I was in the door and about to begin post-mortems with my colleagues, when the phone rang.

Mister McGill?

The most familiar voice in the country.

Yes, Prime Minister.

Misterrr McGill, Muldoon purred. Do you realise ... ?

Yes, Prime Minister.

If ...!

Yes, Prime ...

... my Squad had been with me this morning, you would be in jail.

Yeh, yes. But, Prime Minister, they weren't. (Please, Burton, stop laughing.)

What?!

Er, that's the point.

What point?

They weren't. They ...

Yesss?

Your Diplomatic Squad. That was ... they're supposed ... could we ...?

What?

Could we interview you, Prime Minister, about security?

Just a minute.

Yes, Prime Minister.

White faces peering at me, Burton chuckling.

You there?
Yes, Prime Minister.
My secretary will arrange it.

Next week we waited in reception at the Beehive, Burton drawing a cartoon for the PM's receptionist. Sharon Crosbie emerged. Gave us a sceptical eye. Lesley Miller motioned us to follow her in. The suite, walls and carpet, was an unappealing mustard yellow. I felt as though I had just tried to swallow an unmixed dry dessertspoon of Colman's hot English mustard. Muldoon was behind his desk. He nodded at Lesley. She set up her tape recorder. Burton nudged me. I fumbled with leads to set up ours, on the long, low, blond wood coffee table.

What do you want to know?

Prime Minister, I croaked, are you the only leader of a government who drives to work?

Muldoon looked up from his papers. Hmmm, he said contemplatively. This was encouraging. At least his voice had risen out of deep gravel. Yesss, he said, looking up at the bland ceiling. I wouldn't be surprised if the Prime Minister of Samoa walks to work. Hah, hah, hah. (Uncannily similar to McPhail's Muldoon laugh.)

Ah ...?

Certainly I am the only one I know. Yes.

He is advancing on us. Takes the sofa opposite. I ask him if he has ever talked to other leaders about security, but he seems preoccupied glaring at Burton. No, he growls, still looking at Burton, we don't talk about things like that. I would see it as somewhat embarrassing to my host if I talked about security. It's a very sensitive matter. I always kept off that topic.

He is sitting back, suit open over his ample midriff, his enormous head loose on his hunched frame, his eyes glinting like a boar in a thicket. Why the hell doesn't Burton ask a question, instead of chuckling?

Um, are you worried about a, er, changing mood, in the, um, climate of New Zealand? (That make sense?)

The single problem we have, Muldoon says decisively, is the deranged person copying something that happens elsewhere. We're aware of it, the VIP protection squad and the police. This Trades Hall bombing. The man who attacked Dail Jones a few years ago. He also threw tomatoes at the judge of the High Court and set alight a chair in the court, then said the police had committed perjury because it wasn't the right chair. He was paranoiac. He attacked Dail Jones as a gesture to draw attention to his traffic offence. He is quite capable of attacking anyone – myself, a judge, Jim McLay.

McLay! Muldoon's deputy, his only likely political challenge, so the scuttlebutt around town says. Was there something Muldoon knew, a coded message here? Was I paranoiac? Was the whole country totally under the control of this actually rather small man? Yes, we were. Like rabbits. He was a sibilant snake; we were paralysed, by what we did not know. Fear?

Muldoon was elaborating about some man who thought he had set the security service onto him, heard buzzing from the wall, bugs, was making threats on his life and others, mixing up Gerald Hensley, the permanent head of HIS department, with Bernie Galvin of Treasury.

Frankly, I felt mixed up too, couldn't think which was which. There only ever seemed to be Muldoon, and shadowy figures behind him. He ruled our roost. I asked if there were extra arrangements after a threat like that, hoping this made sense as a question.

Yes! Muldoon snapped.

I sat up straighter. Ah, Prime Minister, I ventured, we know Parliament has had extra security. With the opening of the Beehive. The old messengers replaced. Do you, ah,

11

regard, ah, your driving, as an area of ... looseness? In that tightened ... arrangement? (Was I completely gaga?)

Muldoon was accepting the question, oh, thank you, God, talking about a mental patient escaped in Auckland and his, Muldoon's, home broken into, police thinking it was the mental patient. For a day or two a police car followed me in the morning traffic.

Is Vogel House like the days of Keith Holyoake?

A sharp look.

I mean, could I come and knock on the door?

You could come and knock on the door. (But I wouldn't dare.)

And would you answer the door?

Sure.

And you feel no insecurity?

I have ... hah, hah ... a little peephole. I can look at you and see what you look like.

You don't feel any anxiety driving in every morning on your own?

Well, I enjoy driving. Getting away from either the office or the house. I listen to Morning Report.

My questions began to come more easily. I was relaxing. I learned that Muldoon was woken by a little Japanese watch alarm, that he was seldom late. The day we ambushed him he had had a dinner party the night before. He laughed long and hard at the idea of anybody trying to kidnap him, saying they wouldn't dare. On the contrary, people honked him when he was driving, usually kids, and they waved. When he went to the races or trots, people came up and said, 'G'day, Rob, how are ya, mate?' They might ask him to sign their racebook. He preferred not having security with him; it was not in the nature of this country.

He was not concerned about breaking down on the motorway. He would happily hail a passing motorist. The only difference he saw from Holyoake's era was the planes were a bit faster. He only had this new car because somebody had run into the back of his Triumph in Hill Street behind Parliament. He had had it for nine years and would never have changed. In Auckland he used Norm Kirk's Valiant, which he reckoned wasn't worth much now. There was no extra security built into his Sierra. It did have some buttons he never used, probably stereo.

Security, personally, was no worry to him. His only concern was that some public servants believed they could pass confidential material to the press when they had made an undertaking not to under the Official Secrets Act. He thought security in this country was very relaxed. He had no security inside Vogel House. Indeed, he didn't live in it; he and his wife had a little flat upstairs. There were security lights, but they were there on their own. He was not concerned about having a heart attack and no assistance handy. He did not intend having a heart attack. He hadn't had a day off work, apart from the time in Egypt he was in a dust storm and caught some Eastern complaint. He liked things the way they were, including those four weeks a year at his bach at Hadfield's Beach.

No security there?

I've got the number of the Orewa police station. (The Muldoon neigh, like perhaps the sound of a carthorse caught in a thicket of *pinus contorta*.) No, we're a pretty peaceful country.

Thank you, Prime Minister.

Whew! Lesley escorted us back across the mustard pile. She had allotted us 15 minutes – we had been given 45. I am glad I had a sweatshirt on under the jacket; it absorbed most of the sweat.

Muldoon had had nine years in which to refine his power, his ability to make most of us nervous. I'm not sure he achieved much else. But he was actually more engaging than you expected and certainly a much freer subject on

13

security than the next person I interviewed, Leader of the Opposition David Lange, who was reputedly a better driver. Sean's cover photo captured the Prime Minister with the sun slanting across his huge oval head like a half-cooked egg, which was deceptive, for Muldoon was nothing if not hard-boiled. And a true conservative. I thought his most revealing remark was that he hoped to leave the country the way he found it. To him the country was an old Triumph he controlled and would never swap. He was the reluctant first user of a Sierra in this country, though he rated its performance well, once he had it under control.

Carmen's Counselling Club

Georgina Beyer was interviewed recently on Roseanne's American TV talkshow as New Zealand's and the world's first transsexual Member of Parliament. Carterton's mayor can thank a Taumaranui Maori lad for publicly pioneering man to woman, in the process loosening up one of the last taboo areas. The ironic price for he/she was being hauled before the Parliamentary Privileges Committee for daring to suggest some of its members were bi- or homosexual. This interview came soon afterwards, before Carmen went on to contest the mayoralty of the capital, without success. He was ahead of her time. This interview came betwixt and between times.

Carmen backed away like a Hammer Horror vamp from the afternoon glare, motioning me into her forever twilight coffee bar at the epicentre of Wellington's red-light district.

Oohhh, she gurgled. It's so cold and horrible out there.

The heavy black door swung shut on the wind-blown litter and traffic rush and, above all, the unacceptable daylight. Carmen patted lightly but protectively her glistening black carapace of spray-set hair. She swung about in the stately fashion of a Hollywood duchess in a costume drama, leading the way into the capital's favourite after-hours coffee bar. Her long black satin dress whispered around her ample proportions, the grand circumference of hair bobbing above like a loosely latched motorcycle helmet. Her extravagant chain necklace of pearls as big as bonzer marbles, clacked and swung across her magnificent *embonpoint*, drawing the eyes all which ways, like some mad, speeded-up film of the Marx Brothers at Wimbledon.

From several invisible speakers somewhere in the black

netting of the ceiling Roger Whittaker sang cheerily about leaving some old town. We were outside her customary business hours of dawn to dusk, though in here you would need a well-illuminated watch to know. Carmen, as far as detectable, was unfazed. This was after all her element, the womb-like decor akin to Cecil B. Demille's idea of a pirate's cabin, walls must-heavy with maybe Persian carpets, green glass carboys dangling uncertainly from tarred ropes, blood-red windows, shapely silk shades spilling soft red pools of light over round mahogany tables burnished black and scarred with cigarette burns. A red and black carpet released the working effluvia of tobacco smoke and spilled liquid. An archway hung heavily in gold tassels beckoned punters into a gleaming barrel bar, the inner sanctum. Herein Carmen Tione Rupe, also known in the Department of Statistics and police files as Trevor David Rupe, entertained several hundred hopeful and hopeless, happy and hapless, hog-randy and hung-over patrons with coffee, soft drinks, sandwiches, and Carmen's special kind of unorthodox, inexpensive and in-demand counselling.

We get them all, she said huskily, as she descended with satin sails billowing onto a very bent bentwood chair. We get queers, she said. Criminals. Lesbians. Female impersonators. People with problems, homos, pregnant girls, curious people, drunks.

She sighed, the list no doubt scarcely half-completed. She shifted for a more comfortable position, the chair creaking like rope stretching in the scuppers, and gave her hair a pat check. Worst of all, she said, businessmen. They offer money, ask for a girl, or a pretty boy will do. But no Members of Parliament come here.

She chuckled. On television she had said she knew MPs who were bisexual or homosexual, quite a lot of them; she could name names if she wanted to, but she didn't, wouldn't. Opposition Leader and PM-in-waiting Robert David

Muldoon, another who used the technique of intimating he kept names, demanded in the House 'no less than the consideration you have given a male prostitute'. The demand resulted in Carmen being summonsed before the most powerful body in the land, the Parliamentary Privileges Committee. Wisely, she took along the country's most celebrated criminal lawyer, Roy Stacey. She told *them* she would never have named names. She got a terrible ticking off and was fortunate, with a lot of help from Stacey, to avoid ending up behind bars. To her this is unfair – MPs saying what they liked, the public not permitted to say anything about them.

As well as having the same middle name as Muldoon, Carmen is also a blunt and amusing speaker in great demand, often by the businessmen who might visit her establishment outside office hours. In the previous year she recalled speaking to 10 Jaycee and Lions groups and eight kindergartens. She talked about sex, drugs, transvestites, homosexuals, lesbians and, for the kindy folk, her childhood. She did it to fundraise, for no fee. She wanted to help people. She had always wanted to help people.

In a few years she thought she might become a fulltime social worker. Goodbye to the neon lights, the glamour, the beautiful girls, the minks and furs and flash cars. Her hands waved this way and that and then rose for careful reassurance about her hair placement. She chuckled at the thought of giving up all this, her siliconised breasts shaking like *café-au-lait* blancmanges. Everything about her is OTT, the heavy black mascara thick as tyre strips highlighting the white hubcaps of her eyes. Her full-blown Mick Jagger lips are as red as fire hydrants, set off by a richly creamed foundation. A Polynesian Mae West.

I always wore more make-up than my four sisters put together, she says, more generous than Mae, no side-eye arch glances. I've got seven brothers too, she says heartily. The family's all still in Taumaranui, all married, all straight. But, I get on well with them.

What gets me, she adds, is the condition of the boys I was at school with. When I go home, I see them around town with huge beer guts, missing teeth, no hair, not looking after themselves. They look 10 years older than me, she says, patting her hair briefly.

Where did she get the urge to help others? She thinks it came from her mother, who was a part-time nurse. She practised bandaging on Carmen. I was a model for fractures, she says, silicone wobbling.

We were very close, she says fondly, sadly. Especially after Dad was shot. I was seven. Mum remarried when I was 12. My stepfather was cruel and strict. He fell ill and died. Our mother asked us if we minded her remarrying again. We said we did, so she never remarried.

Carmen levers herself up, the chair as insecure as silicone. She goes behind the bar, perhaps to collect herself, pours hot dead coffee from a Cona glass jug. You become homosexual, she says, if your father is not tough enough. Or not there. The young boy, see, he gets a lot of the motherly touch. It makes him soft and feminine. The kids at school, they jeer at him. So he seeks people like himself.

As a boy Carmen dressed in semi-drag, doing the hula at talent quests, but did not think of himself as a female impersonator until he was 17. The year before that he was seduced by an older man, who eventually died in Mt Eden prison.

I was all hot and flustered when it happened, she recalls. I didn't know what was going on. But I was curious, and I came back.

Carmen became a male nurse in Auckland, until her mother died. She went to Sydney and worked there in a morgue for a year. She answered an ad for female impersonators, learned gypsy, hula and belly dancing, trained as a hostess at Sydney's Chevron Hilton. She then imported this entertaining expertise back to New Zealand, and with it the urge to help the country's misfits and troubled people.

They come to my coffee bar to unwind, she says. A girl tells me she is pregnant; I tell her her parents are good and to talk to them. If she says they've air-raided her, I tell her to go to a doctor. Men come in here and say they're feminine and want hormone treatment. I tell them I'm an entertainer, not a doctor. Women come in all hot and flustered and say they want to become lesbians because their husbands come home from the pub and fall asleep. I tell them to try the She club.

For a decade Carmen has donated $100 or so a month to charity, like Red Cross, the handicapped, the blind. After a hernia operation, she donated a $300 television set to Wellington Hospital. She felt sorry for those patients with no visitors. She gets many requests for help. She paid three months rent for a Northland family when the wife rang to say her husband was sick. She has bailed a lot of people out of jail. Ask the police, she says, if you want endorsement.

I'm never paid back, Carmen says. So I hope God is listening. Send down those angels, Lord. She pats her hair again, saying she was the first to have long hair. Odd? Later the penny drops – Carmen meant she was the first man to have long hair. Inside, trapped in this ample female frame, is that young lad from Taumaranui. And forever trying to escape him. She said she was off back to Sydney for the complete cut-and-tuck operation. Then she would be, finally, all woman.

After my article on Carmen appeared in the *Listener*, minus the cut-and-tuck and other references deemed unacceptable, I received a number of letters objecting to my glamourising this disgusting male prostitute as some angel of mercy. None of them appeared to be signed by

RDM. One full frontal objection came from a mature lady in the office, outraged at this apologist tripe I had written. Perversion was perversion; the Bible was clear about that. Especially Solomon's Song of Songs, I suggested.

Carmen continued to attract controversy in the capital, continued to be drawn to the final female resolution in Sydney. Eventually she stayed there. Years later an old friend of hers and mine, Harry Seresin, also ending his days there, told me he was walking one night in Kings Cross when he was propositioned by Carmen. He reminded her who he was. Carmen apologised, said she had not looked at his face. She needed the money, she said, for an operation.

A Man About a Dog

Murray Ball put The Dog into Kiwi life. In the 1970s Mike Robson accepted for the Evening Post in Wellington Murray Ball's new comic strip, Footrot Flats, about rural New Zealand life. John Clarke had just taken himself and Fred Dagg to Australia. Enter The Dog, its alleged owner Wal, Aunt Dolly and Cooch and a galaxy of Kiwi Animal Farm characters that quickly moved into the nation's newspapers, 26 at last count, then annual book collections, calendars, colouring books, a stage musical, the film, on to 70 or so Australian papers. Footrot Flats quickly became our favourite reading since the Edmond's Cookery Book. Murray stayed put on his Gisborne farm, and that is where I interviewed him up close and personal with his real-life models.

GERROUT! Murray Ball bellowed in a voice fit to crack a farm gate.

The command boomed off round the Gisborne hills, but it failed to have the desired effect. The sheep kept on contentedly poaching grass, its head stuck through his top fence, oblivious to the outrage of Farmer Ball below.

HOI! HSSSSS! GERRROUTTT! shouted an incensed Ball, bounding up his one-in-two hill paddock incline like a goat with old gorse up its bum.

The sheep placidly did not get in behind, not until Ball was pretty well on it, at which point it turned slowly and trundled off.

If it was one of mine, Murray muttered darkly, it'd obey.

Ball has a decibel rating approaching Wal's mustering roar, but unfortunately he doesn't have a dog to back him up. He does have five ewes and two rams on his several near-vertical hectares outside Gisborne, plus a few cows, bees, geese, ducks, hens and a rooster. But in reality they are simply the backrise to his assiduous cartoon industry. He resides not so much in Footrot Flats as Hogtied Heights.

He also has close by two cats and two kittens, but none of the animals have anything to do with Murray rising at 4.30 six mornings a week. He has to get down to his cartoon shed and milk out a cartoon strip, so he can be free when Mason, Gareth and adopted daughter Tania come home from school. Oh, and the wife. His wife Pam is South London, from Murray's successful OE life cartooning for British comics and *Punch* magazine.

The truth of it is, Murray is a bit of a townie about farms, not exactly a number eight wire specialist. When Mason's stolen bike turned up minus the good bits but still functioning, Murray was relieved; he's no good at fixing things. He's still learning how to build a straight fence, coached by two farming lads up the road. They also tell him about bulls, pigs, goats, all the good farming oil. Murray's on a learning curve here as steep as the hill he farms. Last year he did several rounds with a mean goat, won a few battles, lost the war and sold the damned critter after it butted him down.

Not to give the wrong idea. Murray is as lean and fit as any hillside goat. Rugby buffs will recall he was a Junior All Black trialist. He plays a mean game of squash.

The hands but, not nicked and battered and disjointed, no ends missing. They are the soft, supple fingers of a dedicated desk man. His working life as a cartoonist was only possible overseas, there being no training ground here for the wannabe Minhinnicks. Murray wanted to make his way here, but he first succeeded in Britain with his cartoon characters Bruce the Barbarian and Stanley.

Stanley is still a daily chore, for Australia, the States and Canada, and most recently New Guinea. But home is where his heart is, on show daily in *Footrot Flats*.

Murray would never have left if there had been his kind of work here. He was born in Feilding, just like John Fred Dagg Clarke. As a kid there he was copying Donald Duck, imitation being the first stage of development.

Aunt Dolly, he says, is a blend of his mother's rellies: Manawatu landed gentry, Royalist, rightwing, conservative. Father's rellies are actually from around Gisborne, his dad a barber who owned an amusement park and also messed about with farming.

Dad's rellies are scattered around the world, and so was Murray. Part of his schooling was in South Africa where he won a drawing competition, the prize 10 pounds of tea. Back here he began as a cadet journalist on *The Dominion* in Wellington, but most of his copy was drawings. A colleague suggested he concentrate on that. He went back to Feilding to draw, the *Dominion* taking his first efforts. His caveman Stanley first appeared in the *Listener,* its editor Monte Holcroft advising him to stay with his paleolithic hero. He did, taking Stanley overseas.

About 110 strip cartoons later he was still looking for an overseas home for Stanley. He got by grinding out strips for the comic *Beano,* the most punishing but also the most important training. He still does Tilly the Trier for *Bunty* comic and Thor Thumb the Viking in *Topper.* Just once he ghosted the immortal Bash Street Kids. His efforts came back with harsh corrections, but he learned there his distinctive action style.

The two sides of his rellies came out in his cartoons: Bruce the Barbarian in the socialist *Labour Weekly*, All the King's Men in the Tory *Punch.* The two sides got personal when he was living in Devon in the fox-hunting belt. He and Pam organised a petition to build the free state nursery the local squire had rejected. They won. This led to Murray standing on a Labour ticket against the squire. He was relieved to lose, after seeing the council agenda. Much more satisfying was that nearby in Devon lived Frank Pepper, author of those adventure stories in *Rover* and *Champion* Murray had thrilled to as a lad. While Murray admires modern cartoonists like Jules Feiffer, the comics he still illustrates are where the wellsprings of his inspiration lie.

Back here finally, he thought farming the obvious subject choice: barked knuckles from fence posts, the sound fence posts make slipping into a water-filled hole, the sun blisters, the physical effort of shearing. Murray did shear three-quarters of a sheep all by himself last season.

He started with Wal, the businessman farmer all Kiwis know, based on more Manawatu rellies. Next, the tension of opposites. Enter The Dog. The wonderfully intelligent New Zealand sheepdog. Thus the two sides of human nature, the dominant and aggressive versus the softer, gentler. The humour comes from the tugging between the two. Cooch is more like The Dog, based on a farmer friend up the Coromandel. He lives on an estuary island with too much blackberry and trees coming through the floor. Last visit he had two pianos in the lounge.

But animals, Murray feels, are the best way to make a point without putting people's backs up. Anyway, he loves animals. He admires everything about them. The cows are called Rosie and Posie, the ewes Polly, Flopsy and Mopsy. There is Toetoe the calf, Daisy Duck, the kittens Cherry and Apple. Sheba the duck he had to chop; her damaged leg was not healing. He is putting off telling his wife – she loves the animals too.

Animals with attitude he particularly warms to. Like Horse the cat. They don't have to feed him; he brings in eels from the creek. Feel him, I am advised. I do so carefully. His muscles are like plaited steel wire. Even careful scratching of his knobby head is like courting splinters. Murray is proud Horse never backs off from the collies, athough he has had his encounters – a big eye abscess last year acquired while out hunting, maybe for possums. When it rains, Horse lies out in it on the lawn. Yes, Horse may be a bit of a model for The Dog.

Bertie Rooster is another hard case, a black strutting feather duster who periodically unsheaths his claws and chases the children, jumping on backs and getting really nasty. Murray attributes the cluck in his hens to Bertie's performance rating. Murray was told the cluck had been bred out of them. Monstrous! Murray expostulates.

You know ... he says musingly, pausing, a philosophical point rising, probably bound for a comic strip. You know, the news story that upset me most recently, that slaughter of 1000 dolphins. How could they? he adds unhappily, gazing off towards the old white horse Lola in the far paddock. Lola, he says, happily, is out to permanent pasture.

The Empowerment of the Puku

*In 1840 Te Ati Awa No Runga i te Rangi, the Puketapu
from Taranaki, was well established at Waiwhetu, the mouth
of the Hutt Valley. Ten years later they were in decline, their
good land at Lowry Bay taken. When their leader died about
1892, they were so weakened by sickness, depression and
dispersal, like the entire Maori race they were not expected to
survive. At the dawning of the new century at age 18 Ihaia
Porutu Puketapu, their new leader, visited his relation Te
Whiti and learned to fight war with peace, gazed upon Mount
Taranaki and had a vision of a great meeting house at the
head of the fish of Maui that would reconcile Maori and
Pakeha. Waiwhetu Marae was built by Maori and Pakeha,
concrete, wood and glass without, carving and weaving
within. Ihaia negotiated with the government for 23 state
houses around the marae, which opened in 1960, in the
presence of tribal leaders and government officials from all
over the country. One son, Teri Puketapu, is marae builder
and local councillor, while Kara Puketapu became a top public
servant and Maori development entrepreneur, a leader of the
Maori renaissance into the new millennium.*

Kara Puketapu, secretary for Maori Affairs as it then
was and Maori Trustee, tossed a copy of his 1979
annual report across his cool green office.

We had 5000 printed, he says, instead of the usual 150
for the libraries. We wanted people to see what we were up
to, how we were doing.

But do people read this kind of bureaucratic ...?

Look, he says. Let me try to explain.

He slipped a sheet of blank paper off his desk and spread
it over the long, bare rectangle of smoked glass between the

leather lounge chairs. He drew a small bubble with his marker pen, attached a big bubble, wrote the word 'puku' within the big bubble. Then he turned it upside down.

You see, he said keenly, crouched over his illustration with his white-sleeved arms either side, like a fisherman with his hands ready at each end of the eel hole. Here we have the pyramid upside down. The stomach is on top. Why is the puku on top? Because that is the resource, and you merely have the head going in to it. The people make the decisions. It all began to jell when we asked the question: What is the specific role of the department?

Kara Puketapu asks a lot of questions, and answers them. You fall under the spell of this dark, handsome, confident man, grateful you are not an eel, grateful he is not signing you up for a bookshelf of encyclopaedias. Whetu Tirikatene-Sullivan, as Labour MP for Southern Maori, herself from a distinguished political family, called him 'God's gift to the National Party'. This former school dux, former Maori All Black, is a high-powered salesman for Pakeha systems and Maori sensitivities. There was a rumour at one time he would make a good ambassador in Washington, where he is well known from his stint there on a Harkness Fellowship and for his writing on progressive management for the Brookings Institute.

This personable, go-ahead management man arrived in Maori Affairs at a critical time to inject a sense of purpose and enthusiasm into a department and area variously regarded as slumbering or depressed. He believed in economic management as the key. He feels he learned a particularly valuable lesson about the need to tap the people resource, the puku, when he was auditing housing in Auckland for the State Services Commission. All 400 staff had been interviewed, but one stuck in his mind, a girl who had just left school. She said that she thought she had left behind for good the schoolteacher and the rows of desks.

Now she had come to more of the same and she wanted out. He realised she was right, that her environment had not changed, that she was confronted by the school situation, told what to do, not asked to give anything much, stuck at a desk piled with paper.

We put the money into management training, he says, but we hadn't wrestled with the human factor.

He has. When he arrived, his department had the image of a big welfare agency for handouts. He saw it as a farmer, a very big farmer. His management training set him off on an entrepreneurial line of hard investment, getting Maori to manage and develop their land. The result is there in the annual report, profit from land development schemes close to two million dollars.

In detail, his department stimulated market gardening ventures, kiwifruit and boysenberries mostly, at Te Hapua, Helensville and Weymouth, seed potato growing at Ruatahuna, seaweed harvesting in the Hokianga, Bay of Plenty and East Coast. Freezing workers in the Hawkes Bay were encouraged to use off-season time to plant 250 hectares in forest. Over 1000 hectares of new grass was sown. Maori were not just sitting on their land, they were developing it, encouraged by his department, which had a long and close relationship, as distinct from other departments that issued directives and dispensed largesse from a distance. To him it is important not to be seen as the octopus reaching out tentacles into the community, but to be seen face-to-face, making the marae the office. The management word for it is, he agrees, the truly ghastly deinstitutionalisation.

When he trialed the system around Wellington, the only people who turned up were social workers. Predictably, they complained they needed more social workers to do the job. He had not attracted any representatives of the Maori communities, of the puku. He has a liking for organic images. We did an exercise with the staff at district level, he explains, emphasising the need to get out of the hermit crab shell of their own departmental defences. Initially there was anxiety at this self-examination, but now they are excited about their roles.

With the staff ceiling reached, the axe fell on 41. He brought in new faces, from the New Zealand Planning Council, from Parliament, from Waikato University Maori Research Centre. His Tu Tangata programme, headed by Howard Morrison, got pride and purpose into Maori schoolkids, got them striving for higher academic qualifications. There were other community-orientated programmes, like the Kokiri Centre at Lower Hutt, where gang members and unemployed youngsters could come on to a neutral marae and fix cars or weave or whatever. He encouraged his officers to get out there in the community, go to the tangis, mix and advise, help with development of resources, not to offer welfare.

Puketapu was soon getting leaders from all sections of the community at his meetings, looking beyond their own patches. He did a resource analysis, planned strategy. North of Auckland was ready to move into forestry and horticulture. South Auckland was at crisis point. A martial arts expert was brought in to arrange peace talks between rival gangs, while gang members were invited to submit projects for loan assistance from him.

The emphasis with Maori language in schools, he said, moved from demanding it to making the language resource work at local pace and rhythms, not at that of the bureaucrats. Power to the people, power to the puku.

He saw no reason why the same approach should not be tried with other departments of government. Why couldn't Inland Revenue have district meetings to discuss income tax reform? It might learn something! Why not ask parents along to talk about where education is going, not just to be told how their child is doing. The big advantage of community discussion, he says, is that it often throws up something the administrators never thought of. Pakeha call it corporate management. Maori see it as sitting around talking about things.

He has certainly advanced his causes from his own childhood, when all he wanted to do was follow the family tradition into the Gear Meat Company. His father pushed him to university, where he did social sciences. He worked in Internal Affairs, Child Welfare, Justice, State Services Commission, the old DSIR, where he learned to argue with scientists, and spent two years reorganising New Zealand House in London. Unlike most permanent heads, he did not come up through one department.

His conclusion from his varied jobs, travel and Maori orientation is that the manager can maybe provide 60 percent of the guidelines; those managed need to contribute the rest. Management must concentrate on people. It takes time but the alternative, formal organisation, causes inefficiency. Jobs must be developed around people's talents, not people made to fit jobs. Understanding your people and trying to serve them is modern management.

In truth, it is old wisdom, but coming in a fresh fashion from a man who absorbed the lessons learned as a lad about reconciliation and working together. Such lessons stood him in good stead overseas. These lessons have seen his marae at Waiwhetu flourishing. The leadership mantle he has inherited is one that works. In a country that has seen many examples of rags to riches to rags in three generations, we could all, Maori and Pakeha, do worse than embrace his leadership message. After all, it cannot be that bad. It is centred on empowering the puku, reversing the role, turning the heads like himself upside down, with the people on top.

Footnote: Sir Howard Morrison, interviewed on television in April 2000, harked back to his work with Maori kids in that Tu Tangata or self-reliance Stand Tall programme as his most rewarding work, as the start of something.

Call Me Kiwi

Sir Keith Holyoake bestrode New Zealand politics of the 1960s like a truncated colossus. A populist conservative and cunning controller of political infighting, he led National to four straight electoral wins, third longest perch atop the slippery pole after Massey and Seddon. More than that, he made New Zealanders forget the saintly first Labour leaders as he huffed and bluffed and heartily led us through a decade of confident prosperity, sidelining vocal opponents whether duffel-coated anti-Vietnam involvement demonstrators or bloodless opposition or, perhaps most dangerous of all, Rob Muldoon and the other Young Turks within his own ranks. He called on us to 'Call Me Kiwi' and he led from the front, like all those rugby hookers who have developed leadership qualities in the thick of the scrum. I interviewed him in 1976, the penultimate year of four decades in the House.

Sir Keith Holyoake, Minister of State, Grand Old Man of Parliament, held up a splendidly carved wooden elephant. He rubbed its rosewood flanks. Needs a bit of oil, he said. But a fine specimen. Present from the retiring German ambassador, you know. He knew I am very keen on elephants, have a lot of them at home. You've probably heard that story I often tell ...

He leans back in his Parliamentary chair, indifferent to the cubbyhole his new leader and former 3IC Corporal Muldoon has consigned him to. His big, handsome features are heavy with habitual contentment. He knows he has already hooked his audience. He is master of the comfortable, controlling pause.

Cigarette? Noooo? You don't .....?

Of course I don't mind. I am more mindful of his black

eyes, hard as Takaka marble, obsidian, penetrating, almost certainly knowing it is scarcely a decade since I was one of the duffel-coated protesters jeering at his pontifications about standing shoulder to shoulder with our great American friends. Even so, it was only a mild contempt, our hatred was reserved for American President Lyndon Baines Johnson. 'Hey, hey, LBJ, how many kids have you killed today?' was the chant we directed at 'Kiwi Keith' standing amiably on Parliament's highest steps, fondly observing these wayward children ranting at him. Somebody would always shout out: 'Hey, Keith! How high are your built-in heels?' Holyoake chuckled like an old bullfrog, unfazed by striplings wet behind the ears. I still felt wet behind the ears in his presence. Up close he exuded power.

When I was Prime Minister, you see, he said, puffing in his prissy fashion, cigarette held vertically between thumb and third finger, I often used to say that I carried a pretty heavy burden, but ... He takes another puff ... I had learned how to manage. As you well know ... I am sitting up straight, nodding, hoping I well know ... As you know, an elephant is a pretty heavy burden.

I exhale; he inhales.

BUT ...!

I try not to jerk, my knees tight together.

He smiles, a slow, wide bullfrog of a smile. If you begin, you see, when the elephant is a baby and lift it every day, each day it is only a little bit heavier than the previous day. So, you are always able to lift it. Even when it is fully grown. But, if you neglect it for a week or so, well, then of course it gets much heavier to lift, doesn't it?

He is sitting back, his large, bag-encased eyes wide with disingenuous wonder, accepting my metronomic nods of acknowledgment. Game, set, match. Yet there is something deeply phony about the performance, the absurdity of the story, which he has told with enormous relish, placing precise

34

weight and fruity emphasis on every word, allowing his rich *basso profundo* to ebb and flow through the phrases like Rostropovitch's cello bow. Why does one feel a dolt in his presence? This is the man who addressed us graduating teachers back in the early1960s, boasting he had never got past Standard Six and look where he had got to, as if he were telling us our degrees and training were all a waste of time. We knew, the rumour factory insisted, that Keith stood in front of his mirror and practised his timing and putting on the Pommie accent. My flatmate Roger Hall did a wonderful mimic of the old fraud. Keith's mock Maori hakas, eyes bulging, extravagant gestures, we thought him an embarrassment to us all. And yet, when he boomed out 'Call me Kiwi', we accepted, even we disaffected protesters, that he was our own dinkum Kiwi character, our only one, unless you counted Barry Crump.

Here he was, still enjoying life enormously. Last year he had passed 70 and described himself as dangerously well. I could vouch for that. I had been in Nelson receiving some journalistic award and in a crowded room suddenly got an enormous belt in the back. I wheeled around snarling, only to see Kiwi Keith beaming well done. He packed a wallop. I had seen him in the garden of his villa off The Terrace, sleeves up, digging, a man with a back as broad as a kitchen table. And always, even in the garden, he looked smart, as well turned out as any top floor lawyer, sartorially impeccable from the tips of his swept-back, silver-white locks to the ends of his polished wingtips.

He was chuckling deeply. I blinked back to attention. Yes, I know, he confided, that was a bit of an old elephant story. But, it is part of my basic philosophy, that if you train yourself, set yourself a task, any man can accomplish it. Some might be sprinters, some middle distance, others long distance.

Myself, you ask? His eyes have widened again. Well, I

always was a stayer. Slowest fellow on the footy field. Yet, you know ... He is leaning forward confidentially. I lean to accept his confidence. I have, he says, had every possible experience in Parliament.

He leans back, stretches out great sides of hands, enumerates on fingers thick as saveloys: 1931, rookie candidate Motueka, defeated by 500 or so; 1932, rookie member, by 500 or so; 1935, freak win against the Labour tide; 1938, losing member. Bob Semple packed the place with civil servants, true, but, the tide came in, caught up with me.

Pause.

Switch of saveloys.

1943, private citizen, standing for Pahiatua, winning; 1947, Deputy Leader, all those Cabinet posts; 1957, Prime Minister for 77 days, 40 of them electioneering; 1960, leading Opposition back to power. Three more terms. Stepping down to Minister. Back to ordinary Opposition MP. Returning to Cabinet last year.

Out of saveloys. He wheels through the creaking arc of the old, round-armed, oak, public-service swivel chair. His career has come full circle several times. You know, he adds with immense satisfaction, I've never had trouble adjusting to any of these circumstances: successes, defeats, successes.

He unfurls a majestic white handkerchief, a man of massive girth and massive equanimity, at one with all the political seasons, a man of the land. His daughter Diane has married Ken Comber, and Keith has steered him into Parliament. A dynasty is under way.

Even his vanity is somewhat put on. Underneath is something as rock solid as the land he first represented in Parliament. How did he get into the political game, this man of the land? Quite fortuitously, he claims, following the suggestion of a friend after a speech as captain at a footy dinner. He had made reserve South Island hooker, but it wasn't the be-all of his life. The after-dinner speaking was a better bet. Young Keith had the gift of the gab, confirmed when Gordon Coates praised his maiden speech in Parliament as the best he had heard, very generous really when it was by one of his own members opposing his Customs bill.

While talking in the House, Keith also continued to run his farm, unique in the area for growing all the local crops – apples, pears, hops and tobacco. His diversified farm was an experiment that attracted people from far and wide. He says it was undoutedly his defence of the tobacco growers that kept him in Parliament in 1935 and feels it was boundary changes that threw him out three years later. When he returned, he would never be thrown out of the House again.

His immediate solution to failure was a new start, buying a sheep and cattle farm in Dannevirke, but letting it be known he was still interested in politics. He took over from the deceased member and soon was made Minister of Agriculture. In a demanding but rewarding seven years he ran against the tide, making a success of a job that often spelled the incumbent's political death.

How come? The bullfrog smile. I knew farming and horticulture inside out, I knew all the top men, on first-name terms, and I had a good grounding in marketing. I had to dismantle the international marketing department that was so close to the socialist heart and establish producer control. I extended the Apple and Pear Marketing Board process to the Honey Board, the Fruit Board, the Dairy Board. It was quite a job making them all co-operatives, easy to establish, damned hard to disestablish.

He did have the genetic example of the English ancestor who had created co-operatives. He also negotiated well with the Brits, holding good prices for meat, wool and dairy produce. Yes, he confessed luxuriously, he enjoyed the tussles round the negotiating table.

Tussles he enjoys, fullstop. He loved taking National to four wins, especially the last, where all the evidence showed National losing.

I'm a great believer in public opinion polls, he says, pausing for your surprise.

But ...! One saveloy raised. You have to learn how to use them. My friends and colleagues, you know, tell me my political antennae are still pretty good. I was saying all through '75 that National would win.

What was his political style?

Big smile. Consensus. I have no special penchant, except ... pause ... in the smaller ways. I recall two colleagues betting whether I would finish Cabinet meetings before or after six. I wound up business at five to six but kept talking till the dot of six, when the clock was chiming. Then I surprised them by asking which of them had won the bet.

Other smaller ways? Both shoulders rise, as slow and sure as a Russian weightlifter. I've always, he says, pausing, knowing he will elicit surprise, I've always been a most mischievous fellow.

Yes, I am surprised. To the extent that my eyes are widening, like his.

Anybody, he says, a hand waving towards Parliament, will tell you I've always caused more laughter than any other man there, always joking, always a few light words to defuse the more intense moments. Sometimes I've got into trouble because people have not always appreciated my heavy-handed wit, expected me to be serious. I don't think it's necessary, I do think it helped. Like calling for my secretary – then hiding behind the door.

His second name is Jacka, and jackass he is, for calculated reasons. Flossie Burns up in Pahiatua told me another story about Keith, patron of the Scottish Society there, at an ingleside back in '57 or '58, being introduced to a lad, asking his name. The lad said, Sid Holland. And my name, Kiwi boomed back, is Walter Nash. Much confusion from the lad. Later, Keith took him aside and apologised, said he thought he was taking the mickey.

Keith was famous there particularly, but around the country too, for never forgetting a name, an elephantine memory, if you will. Around Wellington the rumour was his private secretary went ahead to check all names in a room and prep Keith before his appearance. In Pahiatua they don't rate that. They still talk about the woman whose name he remembered, and he had not seen her since he danced with her as a young lass. They remember he got the roads sealed and a good quota of state houses. They voted him back 11 times straight.

His secret of success is pretty obvious. Like many an All Black hooker before and after him, he was a natural-born team leader who revelled in the close-quarters work. In Pahiatua it was a pleasure. In Parliament he admits it could be vexing. It took a bit of handling to stop some of the red-blooded young bucks, you know. Tempers did get inflamed. But the greatest satisfaction was leading a team, and holding it together.

When Keith stepped down as leader, the team lost.

Now the team is back in power, Keith admits he still enjoys that, but he does not miss the crushing responsibility of leader, always worrying you might make a mistake, let the team down, and that includes those on the sidelines, in the stands, the hundreds of thousands of supporters. He invited people to call him Kiwi, and they did, and he deserved it.

Right now he was enjoying getting back to what he had missed for so long: the soil, the cabin up on the family farm in Taupo, his own garden down here, the leeks, cauli, cabbages.

Just the one farm you own?

The deep booming symptoms of his all-embracing jollity reverberate like the demented laughter of a stoker locked in the empty scuppers of an oil tanker. The sides of his hands are outstretched, the eyes wide. I own nothing, I am a poor man. Yes, there are five or six family trusts, but they are in my wife's name, my children's. Myself, I own nothing.

Yes, he is mischievous.

A knock on the door. He booms, Enter! Two men enter. Ah, he says, rising, two gentlemen from Auckland, his thick black (dyed?) eyebrows lifting in mock astonishment. Is there such an animal? Well, then how are you, how nice to see you.

And turning to me, huge hand out: And how nice to have met you, young man. He is much shorter, and yet he is much bigger than all of us, his vitality filling the room, the overpowering bonhomie.

I am almost out the door. And don't, he thunders, make an elephant out of me, will you?

I know an order when I hear one. The old bull elephant, maybe no longer leading the herd, but still commanding total respect.

The Black and White Kiri Te Kanawa

Kiri Janette Te Kanawa is our greatest living singer and unquestionably in the top rank of the world's sopranos. I was sent to Sydney in 1976 by my newspaper and told not to come back without an interview with her. Little did I know I had entered the maelstrom of a less public trans-Tasman rivalry, with many in the Australian Opera Company resentful that their own Joan Garden had to play understudy to Kiri. This did not make for the most harmonious environment, except, of course, Kiri on stage in Simon Boccanegra. *The same opera was a highlight of the Wellington Festival of the Arts 2000, but that production did lack one supreme out-front asset, the most stunning operatic star most of us fortunate folk would ever see. Off-stage things were, understandably, a little different.*

The Sydney Opera House on Saturday evening, the curtain rising on Giuseppe Verdi's lesser known *Simon Boccanegra*. Far at the back of the chequer-board stage Amelia gazes out at a painted sea, awaiting her lover. She turns with a swish of much material and sweeps regally down to stage front left. Under an extravagant blonde wig Kiri Te Kanawa's dark eyes flash with fierce love, while the audience gasps with some softer kind of emotion, a sense of awe in the presence of great beauty, a goddess before us in a long white gown trimmed with gold. Almost an angel, anchored to us mere mortals by the earthy passion projecting to the farthest corners of a hushed audience.

She had the wig and gown made in London, you know, the man beside me whispers hoarsely, unable to contain himself. Local costumes not considered suitable.

Shssh! hisses somebody in his ear.

Kiri, obviously in arranged collaboration with the conductor and orchestra invisible in the pit, makes us wait, and wait. And nobody coughs. Some I think are atremble, though that might be me. I cannot be sure; I am trying to ignore all peripheral interference. It is important to keep one's eyes on the prize.

She is singing, a meltingly beautiful aria, her voice high and clear, her flowing gestures weaving out over the audience, touching those delicate and mysterious parts of us around the neck and the backs of the arms and the spine, prickling the blood, raising the hairs. I am scarcely breathing. Then she is finished and there is the crass thunder of pent-up applause, relief and longing already for this fleeting conjunction of vocal and physical beauty of a rare, wondrous order.

Ah, sighs the man beside me, tears in his eyes, she is a beautiful lyric soprano.

Yes, oh yes.

So the opera weaves its sometimes silly spell, the familiar, impenetrable and less-than-motivated court intrigues, the poison, the treachery, the sword, leading with melodramatic gusto to the allegedly longest death scene in the repertoire, even *Traviata* playing second fiddle to the *longueur* of this necrotic embrace. It does not matter. It couldn't. Whatever she does, we are all caught up, like Billy Graham crowds, in mass ecstasy.

My lachrymose informer tells me it has taken four too-long years to get her down here, and for a mere six performances. Then she wings back to Covent Garden, to Paris, Vienna, no doubt the Met, anywhere but back here, her next five years already pencilled in. It sounds so frantic, the life of an opera superstar. A carousel of endless applause, so long as the voice holds up. But she doesn't owe this eager-beaver whinging Ocker her presence, she belongs on the world's stages.

Ah, did you know, she almost had to cancel out because of laryngitis? I trump my informant.

Oooh, he gasps, how did you know that?

I smile, but say nothing. My lips are sealed; I cannot confide in him that I am privy as a guest of the Australian Opera Company to the secret knowledge waspishly whispered to me by a backstage villainess. She almost spat the bad oil into my Kiwi ear. Clearly she was deeply offended Kiri rose from the throaty dead, to die so gloriously on THEIR stage.

But, they just have to lump it, as they did in Hadlee's great era. We for once or twice have the star, so there.

Actually, we don't. We can't afford to get her to New Zealand. Kiri confided later she was dying to come back and perform operas in New Zealand but feared Sydney was the nearest she would get for years. Ah, to be in such global demand.

Actually, it wasn't even easy getting to see her offstage. I kept asking and then begging the Australian admin folk to let me interview her. They kept saying there were plenty of Australians I could interview, considering I was the guest of the Australian Opera Company. Finally, I had to grab the director, a Dane, and tell him that unless I got to speak to Kiri, there would be no publicity from my newspaper for the Australian Opera Company, even though I had a fully researched story. It was cheeky, but I had taken the threat seriously not to return without Kiri in the pouch.

Still there was resistance. I was told I could see her in *Carmen*, though it was probably not the ideal opera for her light soprano; generally you expected a stronger, darker voice. Like an underarm bowling sort of thing?

Lunch was at last lined up for me, then cancelled. I was eyeing the courtesy bottles of Aussie plonk in my hotel room and thinking of drowning my sorrows or going down for another look-see at the incredible collection of nuns' habits, or sails, if you will, that is the other astonishing thing in Sydney, namely, the exterior of the Opera House. I was reaching for the opener when I got the call: Kiri had agreed to hold court in her Paddington pad. It was Sutherland Road, but they didn't say if it was named after their doughty opera Dame, whose voice was amazing but not for Carmen, either. Be there at five pm pronto.

At five pm I found myself sitting in an ante-room with Geraldine from an arts page, music critic Adrian, PR folk, who warned us Kiri was forthright and would accuse us of asking silly questions, and she could swear like a trooper. We sipped the Aussie champers and looked at Aussie paintings of deserts.

Kiri burst in like a police bust, crushing handshakes, then flopped on the floor by the fireplace I can't imagine getting much use in this stifling heat. She leaned her elbows on the glass coffee table. Those huge black eyes coasted like a dark sun across us, eclipsing my carefully rehearsed questions.

Would you, I said foolishly, like a drink?

Kiri's eyes expanded further, which I would not have thought optically possible.

Kia, she said.

Ora, I replied.

I got a tightening of that flawless face for my unintentional facetiousness.

Don't you know Kia?

Um, no.

Cassis and white wine. It's trendy overseas. Like Pimms in New Zealand.

Was she taking the michael here?

Well, she said. Why don't you try one?

Yeh, right, I will.

We all try this sweet blackcurrant brew. I'd rather drink cough medicine. Trendy things often are like that. Still, I had a chance to check her out behind the rim, the white T-shirt with 'Hollywood' stamped across the front, a dark scarf, red-brown trousers. She is not having any bloody Kia, she is pouring herself a tall orange juice. I feel we have lost the first round, and I cannot see us likely to improve, like most of our opening batsmen combinations. The wig has gone, the hair is nicely cut, black, her features are perfect, she is so damned gorgeous nobody really knows where to look.

Whew! she says, relenting, I think, knowing we are a pack of tongue-tied morons. I was so strung up with nerves and stuff last night, she confesses, probably to relax us dweebs. I was, she says, puffing her cheeks out melodramatically, blown out.

I never noticed.

Did I say that? She is arching an eyebrow. She shrugs, pours another orange.

You know, she confides, I do all this for my country, even though you might say I'm detached from it these last 10 years. I'm doing it for the Maori people. They need to pull finger because they are a protected race; they haven't the confidence to get out. I had to make my own trail-blaze. Inia Te Wiata didn't help me, in the nicest sense, in London. He let me do my own thing.

The Aussies look taken aback. So am I. There were all those stories about Kiri being lazy at the London opera school, then Sir Colin Davis just plucking her out of the audition assembly. Mind you, so would I.

I didn't want to be an instant star, she continues, unprompted, unwilling to wait for a dorky, feeble question. I wanted to take a long time. I won't peak in fact for six years. I want to create perfection with the Mozart roles, with *Cosi*, *Magic Flute*, *Figaro*, *Don Giovanni*. Even now no one can touch my *Giovanni*. I am considered for it all over the world. Mozart suits my style and character.

What about *Aida*? The music critic finally comes in with a superior question.

Aida screams, she says with chill hauteur. Anybody can scream.

Is she referring to Dame Joan?!!!

I tend, she says, her magnificently full mouth crinkling at the sides, towards the romantic rather than the dramatic. I want to do the later Richard Strauss, not his *Electra*. Too stormy for me.

I managed to ask a hoarse question about where she lived, cringing at the expectation of its dismissal as silly. She said, with every syllable spelled out slowly, I am settled in Surrey.

Pause. I was thinking her answer sounded like a Henry Higgins alliterative elocution line, like the rain in Spain stays mainly in the plain. Say three times: Settled in Surrey sipping champers by the shallow sea. I wished she would tell me I was silly, just get it over with.

I'm into colours now, she said idly, a sop to this lightweight jerk questioner. And design. Instead of collecting pots and pans. We might move to San Francisco for tax reasons. Switzerland isn't the place any more, restrictions have been brought in.

Adrian asks a complicated question about theatre and opera.

Say again! she snaps.

He does.

She sighs, says it's a hard subject; most producers are horrible. Not Solti. She would sing 'Baa,baa, black sheep' for him, stand on her head. Nobody dares say they would like to see that.

Why do the labyrinthine *Boccanegra*?

For the music. Why else am I in this?

We laugh with collective nerves.

But the plot?

Sorry to be such a snob, she says caustically, but unless you do your homework before ... you see, you have to understand the Italian. We do the death of the Doge with a lisp. A joke. Unless you understand the language, unless you have a ... her fingers click in search of the word ... a fever.

Arts page Geraldine challenges this, says you have to accept audiences find opera easier to follow in English.

Kiri's eyes are flashing, but not with passionate love. Why, she says, her voice anything but light soprano, should we understand only one language? Because we are so bleedin' lazy.

But, Geraldine gasps, you can't expect ...

Oh yes you can.

No, you can't.

You can.

The Aussies have found their voices, and Kiri is not one to back down. After all, she has plenty of practice singing argumentative Mozart duets.

She is scornful of Australia's rugby, racing and beer. If you're going to be ignorant and prejudiced, she says witheringly, then why build the Opera House? Why learn *Boccanegra* in English here when I'm singing it in Italian at La Scala? You're going to have to change if you want to be an international opera company. English is the worst language for singing!

She pauses for a sip of orange across her over-exercised tonsils. Adrian takes the opportunity to make a plea for Benjamin Britten's English operas.

No, she says, doe eyes tossing such a thought aside, they are not my scene. But language is easy. I just did *Eugene Onegin* at Covent Garden. The whole cast begged to revert to the Russian. We did. If you're a parrot, like me, it's easy. I do 40 performances a year, and in between I learn new ones.

How do you manage it? asked Geraldine somewhat reluctantly.

Basically, said Kiri, I'm very strong. At opera school I

was the worst student. I was lazy and bad.

Adrian casts a triumphant glance at Geraldine. Their suspicions confirmed.

I like being bad! Kiri says sweetly. Anyway, the teachers had me in the wrong category. I am a true soprano now. The others blew out their voices. I am slowly building mine up. I take no notice of the critics – a sharp glance at Adrian – even if they cut off my arms and legs. I am influenced only by my husband, my two managers, my singing teacher. The managers want me to do more Strauss, my teacher wants me to do more technique, my husband wants holidays. I might take a year off.

Can you afford to with such competition?

Yes.

Pause.

We wait.

Because I am in demand. Ever since I did the Countess in *Figaro* five years ago.

A lucky break?

Luck starts you, but you have to carry through. You are only as good as your last role. I want to do new ones, make them my own. Anyone can do *Bohème*, but I want to make it my own, as I have with Elvira in *Giovanni*. I have 10 major roles. I want 15, maybe 20 by the time I am 50. But let us be above the rubbish of critics ...!

This was her own Pavlovian signal. Suddenly she unleashed on our pathetic hacks' heads the full-force, high-decibel gale of a *prima donna assoluta* incensed. We were all too busy edging away to the far wall to take notes. Suffice to say she delivered a tirade against critics and the PR fraternity, and it was a humdinger of a tantrum. Nobody could meet those flashing black eyes. I would have reached for more of the alcoholic imitation of neat Ribena, but I didn't trust my pouring arm.

When the storm finally abated, we picked nervously

48

through the debris, looking to divert her heightened feelings. Were not the New York critics ...? Question lapse under the megawattage of her operatic orbs. Didn't Frank Sinatra object to ...? She turned as sharply on the questioning popinjay as *Der Rosenkavalier*'s Marschallin might, caustically informed us she was not best pleased with the publicity shots for *Boccanegra* and had required new ones. There was a rumoured allegation, she sighed heavily, T-shirt heaving, she had said a male singer was nasty. There is hurt in her subsiding contralto. And people were trying to turn her against a soprano, an old friend from opera school days. Kiri was scaling down. Not many sopranos, she groused, remain friends. Diminuendo: I love her very much.

I knew whom she meant from the backstage scuttlebutt, but I wasn't going to say anything. I was too leery of this dame who might be called *La Stupenda* if the name had not already been conferred on an Aussie Dame. How about *La Squisita*?!

Her press agent judiciously reminded Kiri she was due elsewhere, before I guess things got further out of hand. She got up, stomped to the door, then turned dramatically, despite her claim to be more the romantic.

I am in a very incredible scene in opera, she said in a tone fit to play Carmen. It is not recognised in New Zealand. I'm not a country girl made good. I'm working very hard.

Exit one angry soprano. One ravishingly beautiful woman in a tense, bitchy, highly competitive and supremely rewarding occupation. She was a country girl from Gisborne, but Sister Mary Leo honed her natural talents and she went out a young woman and won over the old world. You only have to see her on stage to know why we are all at her feet. Sometimes I guess she is provoked into kicking us, but that's okay. One expects a little pain to be allowed into the presence of such unearthly pleasure.

Now, of course, she has recorded those last songs of

Richard Strauss, available on CD any time I wish to open the portals and enter the nearest earthly approximation of paradise. I have seen the angel, I have seen the devil in her, I now know how I can die happy. I envy Paul Holmes that public kiss, but we can all enjoy her voice. We don't, as Paul's old colleague John Clarke used to say, know how lucky we are.

Our First New-Age Mayor

Michael Fowler was barely a year into the job in early 1976 when my Listener *editor Ian Cross with his talent-spotting eye sent me along to suss out this mayoral windshift in the capital, if not the country. Fowler's predecessor, Sir Frank Kitts, had slumbered along with his city through six terms. While Kitts was trudging around looking for free lunches because he had done the job for public duty not money, Fowler set about improving the pay and sprucing up the city. By the end of his second term Fowler had razed down or raised up the city, depending on your point of view, showing the way for the free marketeering era about to begin.*

Edward Michael Coulson Fowler was, as usual, in a rush. Like some fast new plastic fantastic yacht, he sailed across the plush red, ankle-deep pile of the mayoral ante-chamber, brow ever so slightly knitted with anticipation, anxiety, relish. Left in his wake were the solemn old, stuffy old, varnish-heavy slumped sloops of yesteryear's mayors, shifting slightly on their heavy gold-leaf moorings as he breezed by with corporate striped shirt billowing, unbuttoned, old-boy tie flapping like a pennant, shirt sleeves furled and fluttering with the shifting zephyrs of his busy intent, silvery grey, advertising executive hair tacking over one eye. Here was a mayor in full sail for line honours.

Yes, David, he said breathlessly, with an apologetic smile, I am always terribly ... busy. I only have ... what? ... half an hour before I must meet Barbara. We have this lunch. My wife.

One-eyed he might be, but it was a lively eye, sparkling like a porthole with the sun aslant. He lit a cigarette, eager for everything. I got on with it, knowing he was 45, father of three, distinguished member of established architectural firm, vital, concerned, into projects old and new for increasing the quality of life, saving and expanding the city's soul, his patron saint the go-getting Mayor Crombie of Toronto, who stopped the motorway and rebuilt the city.

I went into politics, he said eagerly, because I wanted to have a little more impact on my city. As an architect I might have built 10 or 20 major buildings in a lifetime.

He waves about, perhaps at the Overseas Terminal out the window, the other way towards the Wellington Club. His firm had done much in the city.

This! he said, encircling the old mayoral suite. This is a way of extending my work – designing a city and its environment.

A vestigial butler serves us coffee from a silver service. We are in cosy, brocade-covered chairs. But Michael is on the edge of his, full of zest for the plans ahead.

I want a third of the inner city saved, he says, his eye bright with fervor. Like the original university Hunter building, the archetypical red-brick pile covered in ivy with grand mullioned library windows looking out over the harbour city, and unthinkably in danger from internal rotters.

This is the big fight, he says with the impatient expectation of an oenophile observing the first pouring of the new season Beaujolais. The university council say it will cost six million dollars to conserve. Our city engineers say less than half that.

Bloody pack of rascals, he adds genially. They know my engineers are right.

That's the conserving side of his programme. On the other hand, he waves out the window, the new town hall design has a lot of form. And it picks up the movement of the sun. The Beehive is unique. The Reserve Bank has a fair bit of modelling. The Wellington Club ...

He leaves it at that, enough examples.

So what are his favourite buildings?

The fifteenth and sixteenth-century villas around Florence. He explains how he has tried to assimilate in his work their sense of enclosure, the internal courtyard, the proportion of wall space to void.

He learned a lot working for Ove Arup and Partners in London, surviving on six pounds a week for the privilege of absorbing what Europe's major engineering consultants had to offer. He enjoyed staying among the Georgian houses of Bloomsbury. His affection for old domestic buildings is reflected in his publications of sketches and histories of Wellington houses and *Country Houses of New Zealand*.

Michael grew up in Marton and Feilding, where his father was general manager of the New Zealand Farmers' Co-op. He went to Christ's College in Christchurch, bringing from there not just English public school affectations and a diffident charm but that city's continuing strong architectural heritage in the form of Miles Warren, celebrated for that city's new town hall and now designing this city's with Michael as architectural patron. Back in those formative days Michael took his talent for drawing to Auckland University, where he became president of the Architectural Society. He had a flirtation with the socialist club there, but felt they used unmercifully his position on the student executive during the wild days of the waterfront strike. It was then he says he got his ideas straightened out.

In 1960 his straightened ideas took the shape of becoming a candidate for nomination for National for the seat of Wellington Central, where Kitts had already sat on his hands. Michael pulled out of that when his wife, Barbara, secretary in his office, was off overseas. In 1968 Michael became a Wellington city councillor and soon came to view national politics as a waste of time, a move sideways that would sideline him, waiting six years for his chance. He says he is too ambitious for that.

He acknowledges most mayors are ambitious, gregarious, with a sense of humour – for without that you have no sense of judgment. He admires the mayor of Toronto, the most political animal he has met. By contrast with this doer and shaker, the English mayors did not impress him. They were meeters and greeters, elected for a year as a reward for services rendered. He thinks mayors should change things. His major aim is to get communication going between council and people, give them a sense of belonging, engender a feeling of parochialism. He plain envies the mayor of Moscow having no financial problems, no ratepayers to tax. Michael admits he is flattered to be asked to write a book on Moscow's planning, at 300 roubles for 24 pages, money for jam with a rouble equal to 87 cents.

Time is passing. He wishes he had more time for writing, but he does have four books on the way, including a novel, a book on acquiring and maintaining property, and *How to Succeed in New Zealand*, a silly title for a satire begun before he was mayor.

He hopes fervently he does not get cast in the role of Establishment. He clearly sees the dangers lurking in the course he has charted for the city, the turbulent waters, the wind-shifts. He feels his major mistake might have been to open up too many fronts. He has taken a roasting from citizens since he invited them to speak up, like those of Makara over rates, Aro Street's stroppy alternative folk over redevelopment plans, city shop owners over a road extension.

There was praise, he smiles, for being the only city mayor to welcome bikies at Christmas – even if they didn't come.

For or against, he got his citizens talking.

While Michael had to be off, the race to the swift, illustrator Bob Kerr and I had to make something of this frisky chat. Back in the *Listener's* calm waters, Bob got it all, the slightly rumpled charm, the enthusiasm barely

54

controlled by diffidence, the eyes bright with bold plans, the cigarette louche in one hand, the other vibrating with the many draughtsman's possibilities for his city's makeover.

Within a year I was a columnist on old buildings for Wellington's venerable *Evening Post* and very much one of those against Michael's emerging plans. Grant Tilly lovingly drew old buildings and I wrote in their praise, and we launched several book collections, at one of which I itemised the third of the 60 or so entries already demolished, a further third under threat. Whilst this squared with Michael's proposal to save one third of the old city, it was the two thirds he was leading demolition of that got a lot of citizens steamed up, provoking many battles, most of which the conservers lost.

Mayor Fowler, no doubt now clearly sighting line honours, led the charge to transform the central city into an earthquake-proof monument to shiny new steel and glass. It seemed there was no stopping the demolition monster he had unleashed, as the grand old houses at the Parliament end of The Terrace tumbled, then the cute Victorian wedding-cake shops on the crescent of Lambton Quay.

I stood on an oil drum and harangued a lunchtime crowd about this desecration, but they couldn't hear me for the noise of diggers and demolishers. Architect historian Chris Cochran planned to not just sit in but live in the old Midland Hotel, our only Spanish American hotel. It went. So did the stately State Fire. The demolition ball headed like something out of HG Wells up the Quay, taking out the gargoyle-groaning Colonial Mutual, up the Willis Street pub row, along Manners Street intent on bowling all of the inner city. Mayor Fowler defended vigorously all demolition of buildings he dismissed as second rate and not worth keeping. His Labour councillor opponent Keith Spry had to enlist endorsements from the likes of Leonard Bernstein to save the old Town Hall, as the new one rose like a concrete cockroach beside the splendid old Victorian pile.

And yet, and yet, Michael was still doing his charming sketches of old wooden buildings, one of which he lived in in the old wood suburb of Thorndon, part of it declared the country's first protected suburban precinct. And the Hunter Building was saved, and so was the Mission to Seamen Building, where Chris Cochran and friends did sit in and perhaps took on an easier adversary, the government of the day.

When the dust finally began to settle, due largely to the economic boom disappearing into the dark deep hole of the '87 crash, Wellington was a pitted and pitiful mix of old and new. And yet for many this was a revitalised city, the café culture beginning its amazing surge, the waterfront now the focus of all the plans and conflicts about old and new.

Sir Michael, as he now was, maintained his mix, sketching and writing fondly about old wooden buildings and new architecture, notably in his attractive 1983 volume *The New Zealand House*, a book I continue to enjoy. While he was putting that together he also, with effortless facility and considerable charm, wrote a column on restaurants for a magazine I edited. There was no disdain or resentment of my frequent attacks on his civic policies. At the launch of the book in his new town hall, the Michael Fowler Centre, which I had likened in print to an upended stainless steel colander, allegedly his first name added to avoid it being dubbed The Fowl House, Lady Fowler said amusedly she was always a little anxious about me and my wild-eyed conservation attack-tics. I said I was always a little anxious of her husband. Yet it was in avuncular fashion that he offered me advice to stop my magazine's reviews biting the hands of those restaurants that could feed us our advertising lifeblood. Alas, it was too late, the magazine folded and I moved on to edit its lapsed column on local suburbs.

Then I spent a year in Auckland where, to my surprise, Sir Michael was urging similar policies of urban renewal. I wrote one of my wild-eyed letters to the *Auckland Star* warning about this knight in shining armour on his white charger aiming to bowl old Auckland. I went back to Wellington and the *Star* folded. Sir Michael, serene in the City of Sails, pushed on for further line honours.

A decade later I was back in Auckland writing about old buildings that had been saved and restored, like the Chelsea sugar factory complex, including the wonderfully refurbished old wooden workers' cottages on the estate. The architectural consultant was Sir Michael Fowler, still mixing his zest for the old as the new.

St Peter of the Kiwi Skies

Peter Button was the first air ambulance rescue pilot in New Zealand. He paid for the helicopter himself in the mid-1970s, and then fought through two decades the bureaucracies that sought to close him down. He had saved many lives, notably in the dangerous Cook Strait waters, before he lost his own on a police job tracking an escaped prisoner when his helicopter struck wires he had himself laid. He established the now nationwide rescue helicopters, but he died as too many good pilots before and after him have from the failure of our bureaucracies to install warning coloured balls on power lines often invisible to the magnificent men in their eggbeater flying machines. His nickname was St Peter, he was a local and sometimes national hero, he was a chip off the old pioneering block of resourceful Kiwis who see the need for something and nothing and no one stops them filling the gap. Nobody has quite filled the gap left by St Peter.

On 2 July 1986 the police launch *Lady Elizabeth* was on a training run in Cook Strait, tacking toward the Eastbourne coast. Wind was gusting up to 130 kph with five-metre southerly swells, showers and some hail, but the boat was designed to cope with these conditions. Nothing can be done to plan for the freak wave that rolled up the channel and rolled the boat off Barrett's Reef.

It was one of those days I didn't expect to be flying, says Peter Button in his typically underwhelmed Kiwi way. With the wind at 60 knots plus it was not a day you fly because you want to. Planned programmes had been abandoned.

Then the beeper he carries night and day went off and he was running to a phone, to learn that the police launch had capsized with four men aboard, several his constant colleagues in many Cook Strait rescues. One look at those seas, he says, told you any boat that came alongside those men would kill them. The Bell Jetranger with its winch was the only means of saving them.

It took him a too-long quarter of an hour to get to the airport, on the way picking up his son Clive, his winchman.

Everything in this situation has to go right, he says. You don't have a second chance. And it wasn't a day for learning.

The faintest of smiles crossed his long, thin mouth. This lanky, silver-haired man of 56 has that relaxed look James Coburn made famous in *The Magnificent Seven*, the look our All Blacks of old maintained at critical times to avoid defeat. A former basketballer, plumber, real estate agent and insurance broker, he is now a helicopter pilot enjoying what he calls his second childhood. He is as direct and unpretentious as the spartan cafeteria we are sitting in, the airport office of his Capital Helicopters over the unfashionable side where the big Air New Zealand unsilenced jets reach maximum thrust and mind-scrambling scream. A milk bottle stands by the Zip on the formica bench. Peter is dressed in his working clothes: white shirt, blue trousers, tan shoes. His eyes are as straight and direct as the line of concrete tarmac through the window, blue as the skies can be overhead on a good day in three. He does not blink.

We took off into the southerly, he recalls. My son was standing on the skids below. I'm a bit of a fatalist about flying with my son. What will be will be. I like to think if anything happens, it won't be through any fault of mine. You're going out to solve problems, not create them, though I sometimes think of the engine failing and the drop speed of 2000 feet a minute. It would all be over very quickly, particularly when you are virtually at sea level.

This day they located the *Lady Elizabeth* quickly. His problem was that flying over water is difficult in the best weather, and helicopter flying is by sight. Unless you have something to lock your eye on, it is hard to hold a position over water. It is very hard when the people in the water have disappeared from your sight and you are relying on instructions over the intercom from your son standing on the skids, covered in spray just above wave height. Another freak wave at this juncture would have taken the helicopter.

You don't look at your watch in such a situation, he says. But I suppose it took about 10 minutes. When we got there I knew the men in the water, one face down. We winched them up, then I went out with the scoop net to recover the body. After a couple of tries I managed to. It was probably half an hour before the three of them were back on land. One of the two men alive was pretty gone.

Launchmaster Senior Constable Jim McLean and crew member Constable Rod Herd were saved from certain death, and probably by minutes.

The phone rang. Button was wanted. Five minutes later he was in the air, a policeman aboard, tracking a man loose with a gun wandering the city.

I'm almost an honorary cop, he said on his return. Yes, we got the gunman.

Nothing surprises him anymore. He works for the police, for the firemen with a monsoon bucket, ambulance work. A third of his workload is emergency related. He was the first here to develop a full support medical unit he can take at any time, along with doctor and nurse. Typical is spinal transfers to Christchurch, which is a crucial one hour 45 minutes away compared to fixed wing flight and road transport of six to eight hours. Button is the only rescue pilot in the capital, working out of this shack.

What prompted his rescue operation was watching helplessly from Seatoun as the *Wahine* foundered off Barrett's Reef with all those lives lost. He bought his helicopter before he could fly it. The air inspectors who would decide what he could do with it had no helicopter-flying experience and applied fixed-wing standards to this infinitely flexible machine.

Button had been involved for years in ambulance work before this, but of course in fixed-wing planes. He had learned to fly on this very tarmac in 1949, having been born and bred and a plane spotter up close in adjacent Miramar. He had seen air pageants as a lad, including the one where a parachutist fell to his death on Lyall Bay beach. He points to the hillock from where he witnessed the death.

Too young to go to war, Peter missed out on a flying job because of all the ex-service pilots in the queue ahead of him. So he became a plumber, a real estate man, an insurance broker to feed his young family. He had to settle for the aero club.

Tiger Moths and Chipmunks were just not enough. He kept trying to get a commercial pilot's licence, stumbling at the red tape because he didn't have School Certificate, which ignored his 90 percent maths average. It was the shape of his hassles to come. I guess, he says with his thin smile, I attract fights.

He was 27 when he got his commercial pilot's licence. Air New Zealand rejected him as too old. Two years later they were employing blokes of 28, but by then he was 29, again too old. Catch 22 stuff.

I pottered, he says, doing commercial air charter work for the aero club.

In 1975 he formed Capital Helicopters and then the bureaucratic battles began in earnest. He could not get an Air Service Licence; it was a closed shop. No licence if somebody claimed it would jeopardise an existing service. The result was lives lost, as when a man was shot at the back of Wainuiomata and the helicopter ordered from Christchurch could not arrive before dark. The *Wahine* passengers dying, Button watching helpless.

It took $50,000 and many months later but he got the licence. The inspectors wanted it restricted to a 30-mile radius of Wellington. He ignored them, flew to Levin, on to the Magistrate's Court, then the Appeal Court. He would like to take it all the way to the Privy Council, just to prove his point of principle. These bureaucrats, he says in his matter-of-fact voice, claim they are acting in the public interest. They are simply acting on whim. They have forgotten the reason for aviation. I would hate to put a figure on the unnecessary cost to us and to the country of bureaucratic delays. Like the two years and huge legal fees trying to get an amendment to the Air Services Licences to put in a similar service in Auckland. We were knocked back and treated with ridicule and like criminals.

You can see why he stood for the New Zealand Party at the election. He hates quangos, he hates quasi-judicial authorities. He thinks the State needs to be reminded that its role is to establish and maintain social order, not to tax him out of existence. The most incredible tax came from Customs, tens of thousands of dollars required to pay for the privilege of piloting police and doctors on search and rescue and casualty missions – those who seek your help in matters of life and death, and you have to pay the government to fly them!

Amazingly, his humanitarian spirit is unscathed. He says his original aim was to find enough commercial work to be able to maintain the emergency operations. It was a constant struggle, with the authorities even frustrating his commercial operations, refusing him a licence to carry building materials. The Westpac sponsorship arrived in time to allow him to continue saving lives.

The bureaucracy has no interest in the value of saving lives. The Germans have established that a helicopter saving two lives each year pays for its capital and running costs. Saving Rod Herd and Jim McLean, who are back at work, saved ACC huge sums in widow and child support. He finds ACC very slow in paying his bills. Or the man Button picked up from Wanganui after a bulldozer rolled on him. Button is taxed by Customs for taking the doctor and nurse to the injured man. He is at death's door. Ten days later he is home. Button is out of pocket for this job. He says the money all goes into the other end of campaigning to stop accidents, when lives would be saved if there were the American approach of getting victims to hospital within an hour of trauma.

Button still offers a better service than anywhere else in the country, doing jobs few would want. Worse than the *Lady Elizabeth* was flying into a 75-knot front at night to search for kids missing off Kapiti, or going out to the *Mikhail Lermontov*. On night flights over water, he says, you feel particularly vulnerable. If anything like a wave-drenching of the rotors had happened the day of the *Lady Elizabeth* rescue, there would have been the death of him and his son to add to what would have been four casualties from the boat. He has ordered a two-engined helicopter because it covers the risk better than one. He was banking on a contract to fly Harbour Board pilots out to ships to pay for this. He took up the Harbour Board chairman and a visiting expert to look at the proposed port development. Then the Harbour Board awarded the contract for harbour pilots to a Nelson firm without Button's experience of Cook Strait conditions. The contract was the bread and butter that would have justified the million dollar two-engine helicopter.

It bloody hurts, he says. We needed that bread and butter. I had hoped to have several more helicopter pilots working with me.

It might have saved his life, if he had concentrated on rescue work, not been distracted lifting poles to earn enough to continue rescue work. You could argue he was killed by the Catch 22 of the way the authorities handled him.

Over the other side of the airport they make massive profits. This side, Button saved those in peril for bugger all. He was not bitter. He considered himself a lucky man to be doing what he loved, enjoying good health, proud of his skills, of the lives they saved. Little wonder his nickname was St Peter. God bless.

The Man Who Dressed Up the Police

Rob Moodie is remembered as the police advocate who wore a dress. When I first met him in 1976, he was Dr Robert Moodie, barrister and senior lecturer in law at Victoria University of Wellington. Roll-top white sweater under the jacket, sideburns, clean shaven. Later that year he changed jobs and changed into a dress, or more accurately a kaftan, in which he pushed very hard for better pay and conditions for those who employed him, the New Zealand Police Association. Not only did he move the police from the bottom to the top of the Public Service pay and conditions ladder, but he was one of the few public figures to speak out publicly against the other Rob, most particularly against Muldoon's policy on the Springbok Tour. The last time I saw Rob he was in conventional gear farming goats out of Feilding, his extraordinary public ambition to change the way the police and society viewed each other triumphantly fulfilled.

A doctor of goats was visiting from Texas; millions of dollars were involved. Thus, I had only 'x' amount of time, Moodie explained briskly, sitting in his simple office behind his Feilding home.

The dress?

A useful ploy, he says. Part of the negotiating strategy.

Goats are now the total focus of a moustachioed man captured by the *Dominion* photographer cutting the ribbon to open a men's boutique in Wellington, wineglass in one hand, scissors in the other. Between, a flowing dress with laced edges and an elaborate floral embroidery across the chest, set off by a gold chain around his neck. The dress is long gone. The man hasn't really changed, direct and forthright, hair thinning a bit more, same disconcertingly direct stare behind the same black horn-rimmed glasses.

Fibre goat farming, in a way, is the full circle for a man who has always been in both a physical and intellectual hurry, intent on righting wrongs and achieving his goals without wasting any time. It is not so much that he is unconventional, as that the rest of us are stuck in our ways and he is moving along with whatever works. Robert Alexander Moodie was born at Port Chalmers and started running early, away from an unhappy home. He ended up a state ward for several years, brought up by a farming family near Oamaru. At last, something useful to do. He was managing a farm by age 18.

Waitaki Boys' High School gave him the private schooling that set standards, but he rushed from that to work that would use up his huge energies: the freezing works, contract fencing, farm labouring. His encounters with the police were not initially voluntary, sharing the local constable's vehicle as he was returned to his reluctant home, sometimes including a stern talk about stealing bikes or comics. Local Senior Sergeant Fred Leadley is the kind of policeman we always need more of. Instead of locking up stroppy Rob, he gave him a job, escorting other kids doing a runner from Child Welfare. Fred chatted about his job and Rob got interested. In 1959 he joined the police.

Naturally, Rob was not going to settle for pounding a beat. He got accepted into detectives, arriving for work in a green suede waistcoat and matching shoes. This was the era of the plainclothes police in very plain clothes indeed. Rob drawing attention to himself was frowned upon. But, he got results – his nickname, 'Ace'.

School had not been his thing, but the reason had not been identified by a system and a society more interested in obedience than anything else. Rob found out for himself he needed glasses, and with them came a sudden surge of interest in reading. This drew him up the hill to study for a law degree part-time. Although he had fast-tracked to inspector, it was not enough; now he wanted to read and study. In 1972 he resigned from the police to study law.

He studied so well he became senior scholar and was offered a lectureship. It took four years to get his doctorate, along the way winning a 1973 prize for the best contribution to legal writing. He published articles and became a current affairs commentator. A legal career beckoned abroad, teaching jobs in Australia and Canada on offer. But this was dull stuff. He wanted to do something more exciting, more significant, more at the coal face.

As he told me then, the state had too much power, due to the lack of any balances and checks like the two-tier British and Australian systems or the American-style separation of legislature and executive. Neither major political party in New Zealand wanted to change the rules. Judges took advantage of the concentration of power. He noted one recently ajudging a traffic officer could chase you on to your property to give you a breathalyser test, the idea your home is your castle giving way to the road code. He said courts did not decide strictly in accordance with the law, but with the judge's view of the case, using the law to justify the view.

This problem with the law could become a matter of life and death, as he argued in a journal article. It was prompted by a man in Christchurch knifing a girl in the neck, the police hesitating to shoot because the target area was his head. The official policy was to shoot to wound, but Moodie would have none of that. You shot to stop a mortal situation, to save lives. If somebody died as a result, tough.

It was this stance that helped get Moodie back together with the police, as their industrial advocate. Moodie had already as a lawyer been consulted by a group of police interested in getting rid of their ineffectual representative. He had even represented one member accused of abusing the Police Association president. A policeman tipped him off about the Association job coming up. He got it, and the dissident police probably thought they had their man in place. As it happened, Rob had much more revolutionary plans.

Moodie wanted to change the way the police were controlled, and he wanted the police to change their view of the society they were sworn to protect. Moodie soon found his flashpoint, a constable shot in the stomach in the line of duty and languishing seven years later without compensation, not helped by his elected representatives or the police hierarchy. On the contrary, many viewed this crippled man as a malingerer. Rob went in to bat for him, bat being the operative word, Rob batting words about the heads of those who had the power to help and had done nothing. The injured policeman had a house built for him.

Rob realised the policeman had received no help because nobody in the police knew how to negotiate the bureaucratic system. This was a specialist field, a minefield if you like, of pettifogging rules and regulations and little milk of human kindness flowing among the enforcers. Rob found the whole system of police representation like a rudderless ship, drifting about without any control and without getting anywhere. Rob was uniquely qualified to do something about it, and he wanted to. A policeman had put him on the right track. He set about putting the police on the right track. Being Rob, it was a very fast track.

Unlike his predecessors, who did not trust the media and did not feel comfortable appealing to them, Rob ignored the strait-jacket job description he had signed up for, and the first day in it went on telly to demand the police pay claim be settled. The old guard were horrified and told Rob he had spoiled all their careful work. The young police loved it. Rob toured his constituencies, attracting crowds of angry young police, attracting publicity wherever he went. He publicised the level of discontent so well the politicians got the message and settled the pay claim. In the process he virtually cut out the chain-dragging middleman, the police commissioner. Naturally, this met with an indignant response, but it had never been Moodie's nature to back off from authority. He confronted the commissioner and stated his policy, then carried it out, basically going straight to the Police Minister.

Moodie was in his element. The police were prevented by law from being a trade union, so Moodie did the job for them. He ignored the grumbling about lack of consultation and got on with getting a better deal for members. He brought in top academic research officer Graham Butterworth to arm him with the factual anomalies with which he lambasted the bureaucrats. He recognised that without the strike threat you needed good material argument. He also realised the police were their own worst enemy, or at least their bosses were, refusing to change as society did, still trying to impose their buttoned-up ways, refusing to let policewomen wear trousers, as a for instance. Rob solved that problem by wearing a dress to his meetings with the police brass, taking along his wife's necklace for good measure. He started wearing a kaftan to the office and on television. It was to shake up the complacency all around him, the complacency that found reasons not to do anything, like helping that injured policeman.

When policemen suggested he was queer for wearing a dress, Moodie said he was not sure about that himself. Wind out of uptight sails. When there were official complaints, Rob was pleased to see the majority of the force supporting him. They had had enough of being told to get a shorter haircut. Rob had fun with the dress, and he saw how it liberated the thin-lipped blue line. The cartoonists helped; all the publicity about a man in a dress had its effect in relaxation of dress codes in the police.

Rob took his campaign a step further, questioning the

society that was so over-regulated it could not tolerate difference, that wanted the Polynesian to change into the European-approved image, but the European was the problem, not the Polynesian. So many Europeans drank too much because of the frustration of their authoritarian society. While some police took issue with this nancy boy garbage guff, Rob was also turning around the police family situation: larger families and under eight percent owning homes against a national average of 28 percent, with inadequate life insurance.

Moodie and Graham Butterworth adopted a five-year plan to improve all salaries and then improve early retirement, superannuation and sick leave. Their biggest problem proved to be the procrastination and hostility of Treasury and the State Services Commission, who did not accept the police had a case for margins to be increased, given they could not use the ultimate workers' threat of the strike. Moodie relished this huge battle, which he won. But in the process his uppity ways made him and his members an enemy in the top dog.

Rob Muldoon expected the police to toe the line. Here was Moodie drawing a new line in the sand and tugging government over it. The police were even challenging policies such as the dawn raids on Polynesian overstayers. Then the Association brought a case alleging bias against the government-appointed commission into the Arthur Allan Thomas conviction and expressed concern the police would be blamed for any decision on the Springbok tour and wanted to be involved in any planning. The Association technically perhaps won its bias case but incurred huge legal costs and attracted the ire of the prime minister. When Muldoon let the Springbok Tour go ahead, Moodie had his members divided about 60 for, 40 against, like much of New Zealand. In this bitter and divisive tour he defended the police as the meat in the sandwich and stood up to

Muldoon, saying he felt he had in some sense encouraged the tour.

At times it seemed Moodie was the only national figure prepared to square up to the pugnacious prime minister. Internally he continued to encounter vocal opposition from several men who went on to become National Party Members of Parliament. Rob maintained the Association must have a social conscience, that on the overstayers in particular the police should not be seen as pursuing them like birds of prey.

Moodie was the calm helmsman through these stormy waters. He believed the Springbok Tour finally showed that police as reactive agents were confrontational, that police should work with the community to defuse problems. The outgoing Police Minister was unrepentant, advising them to put the boot in. Moodie countered that this was criminal and could put police in gaol.

Although he was aware his members thought him a Labour man when in fact he was a member of the National Party, this did not stop Moodie with professional pragmatism lobbying Labour. Once Labour was in they dithered a bit, but Moodie and Butterworth nudged them into the early retirement approval as a way of rejuvenating the police. By early 1985 the mission was accomplished, and Moodie proposed an end to his job in favour of a fully professional operation with three people to replace him.

Another way of seeing it was that one man did the work of three. In a decade remembered largely for a negative prime minister, a man in a dress improved police pay and conditions out of sight, and with it their morale and a willingness to work with rather than to confront and control those they should protect. It was one of the most extraordinary periods in New Zealand's history, perhaps the closest with the Springbok Tour clashes that we have come to outright civil war. There was no question some in the police would have welcomed this opportunity to sort out with the infamous long batons those pesky protesters with no respect for their traditional authority. There were others in the police who objected and even refused to confront their own families on the protest lines. With a more traditional man in Rob's role the police could well have gone down the path of Rob's Mob, as the Prime Minister used to call his imagined constituency. Anti-mob Rob led the call for the police as mediators.

In everything he did as Police Association secretary he was consistent, committed, compassionate. Pity he didn't want to lead the country. The full story of the intricate negotiating path Moodie took is detailed in the history of the New Zealand Police Service organisations, *No Right to Strike*, which I was privileged to be commissioned to write in the early 1990s.

Along the way many of his own members went on about Rob's ego as well as his dress. For him, none of that mattered; the only thing that counted was social justice, ending a system that could victimise a policeman shot in the line of duty. Moodie succeeded, and was content to get on with a return to his farming roots, having repaid in full measure the policeman who helped him, leaving New Zealand a better place for both citizens and police. One can only pray that President Putin has a five-year plan that will work as well for Russia, whose morale is not unlike that of the police when Rob Moodie came into the job.

The Grand Old Man of
Kiwi Motoring

*The Southward Museum above Paraparaumu is world famous
for arguably the best vintage car collection anywhere. It is as
big as an aircraft hangar and packed with the full range of
vintage cars you see streaming through southern England in
the Brighton Rally immortalised in the British movie
Genevieve. There is a basement garage containing even more
vintage cars. This surely is car heaven. It spans the 20th
century history of motoring, as does Len Southward, a living
slice of world history on wheels.*

Len Southward is a courtly old man who is happy to
take you on a conducted tour literally and
metaphorically down his memory lanes. Goodness
knows, he has done it a thousand thousand times. But when
you are passionate about your work, when your work is your
hobby, your life, your reason for living, it is no sweat.

I borrowed money from my mother for my first bike, he
says, gazing fondly over a convention of venerable two-
wheeled machines. He is not talking about a push-bike.
Len was born to ride motorised machines. She was a 1908
Triumph 500 three-and-a-half, he recalls. Fixed engine. You
know, the kind you had to run and jump on.

Indeed, I did. My first motorised transport was a brute
of a Standard motorbike, which you ran to start because
the kickback on its foot starter was likely to take your foot
off. But Len is talking about pre-footstarters.

The Triumph was only his first purchased motorbike.
He was playing about with bikes before he was a teenager.
Yes, push-bikes. But he read all the motorbike magazines,

cobbled together plugs and engine parts and turned his push-bike into a motorbike.

There was only one job Len wanted. At age 13 he started at Inglis motor warehouse in Taranaki Street, where Lucas became established for many years. His pay was two pounds a week for 44 hours. He swept out the showroom at 8am, ran messages, answered the phone. The numbers were 2441 and 3001.

His memory is great, his chat non-stop, and that includes answering the phone which never stops ringing, coping with printers calling, somebody wanting metal tubing, the local library after vintage car history, men from the workshop with mechanical problems. Len is red faced, but not from stress. He has some white hair left, but that is age and not worry. Len is coping with everything – a tall, lean authority figure of almost Biblical charisma, gentle as Jesus, bold as Moses.

Inglis specialised in the Republic truck, he says, putting the phone down and shutting the door. Its grille was like a Daimler's, a squirrel inside the wheel was the trademark. There is not much interest in them now; people prefer the cars and bikes they knew personally. He had located one Republic truck being used as a water tank at Trentham. The problem is, Len is the only guy still around who would have recognised it.

A china His Master's Voice dog has its head cocked in his direction. On the wall behind him is a vintage Fiat poster. The rest of the place is teeming like a Steptoe and Son junk yard with specs and parts for bringing all Len's old motors back to pristine condition.

Len was born about the same time as the motorcar. In 1920 at the age of 15 he assembled an ABC motorbike for a returned soldier. He still has its registration papers, and the bike, which he had to reassemble. He opens the door to point out where it stands between a 1929 Harley

Davidson and a rangy old Indian complete with leather thongs around the saddle bags and tassels on the back of the seat. Nearby is a Brough Superior, the Rolls Royce of motorbikes. Len knows – he wound it up to 180 ks an hour at Otaki Beach a few years back.

From Inglis Len went to the Williams car yard at 20 Arthur Street, off Cuba Street, which the Ministry of Works took over. He worked there on the Thorneycroft Model T trucks for Murphy's brickyard and on local cars. At the time he lusted after the Minerva cream roadster owned by Dr Robertson of upper Willis Street. Now Len has several Minervas.

Motorbikes back then were still his passion and he went to work for Harley Davidson agents Rodgers and Hall, opposite and up from the YMCA at the top of Willis Street. From there he moved down to Sutherland and Rankin in Mercer Street, opposite the *Evening Post* building. They were agents for the Indian motorbike.

By this time he had sold his Ariel for 23 pounds at Tawa Flat and acquired in 1924 an AJS for 80 pounds, which he cranked up to its numerical cost in miles per hour at Otaki Beach.

In 1926 he set up his own motorcycle repairs in Lorne Street, near the present Greek Orthodox Church. In 1930 he moved out front to Kent Terrace, next to the Elliott heritage brick house. Five years later he switched to cars. Kent Terrace remains *the* car yard strip in Wellington.

Len rebored a Baby Austin for seven pounds 10 shillings, and did an engine overhaul for under double that. He repaired Morris Minors, Austin 10s, Dodges, Chevrolets. He spent a night reboring Sam Bowler's milk delivery Dodge so Sam could do his Makara run in the morning.

During the war Len couldn't get muffler tubing so he made his own. This was the start of his NZ Tubing factories in Auckland and the Hutt Valley, with a staff of about 250 managed by his two sons.

Why the museum? That was inspired by seeing a veteran car rally in Birmingham in 1955. He came home and bought a Model T Ford for 40 pounds. It is on display in his museum, in all its inglorious rust, the way he found it. Len bought another Model T, then a Swift, a Darroch, a Holsman, and by then the bug had bitten.

In 1972 he set up a museum trust. Today you can see half of his collection of over 200, all apart from the Model T, in superbly restored condition. It is a stroll through a more graceful and leisured age, with the big engines, big bodies, big running boards of the glorious old Lagonda, Benz, Vauxhalls, Wolseleys, Stutz, Cord, Marlene Dietrich's Cadillac, Hudson, Phoenix, Bugatti. He knows every one of his venerable vintage beauties, including the most intimate details of what is hiding under the bonnets.

In the basement garage the beauties are revealed in various stages of *déshabille*, like the 1923 Gwynne, maybe the world's first automatic, and the incredible Mercedes 540K, of which a model was sold recently in the States for almost half a million dollars.

Len would never sell; he only buys. The purchases include cycles, old planes and traction engines. There is even that Kiwiosity, the backyard, orchard-spraying wooden contraption, which he picked up for $50.

The intercom has burst into life, demanding Len's attention. Some folk from Liverpool are also after him, trying to fight through the half dozen business suits. The demands are incessant. Len, as a friend says, is riding a tiger. He would prefer an old Indian or a Harley Davidson, the throttle wide open, the long stretch of Otaki sand ahead. Nowadays he has to settle for the sedate 1912 blue Buick. It is out there; he drives his pristine vehicles off the showroom floor and back again. You can never have too many. Len has not died but has gone to vintage car heaven.

The Kiwi Choice for Our
Most Pleasant Voice

Relda Familton appeared a few years back on the **Holmes**
Show *and startled the nation by removing her wig to reveal
the baldness caused by her fight with cancer. There were tears
in our eyes at her brave gesture of flinging aside the taboo on
this hitherto concealed side-effect. She lost that battle to cancer
soon after. But she is remembered fondly as the soothing and
sympathetic late-night voice on National Radio, and before
that as a popular broadcaster and television presenter. Relda
was from that era when local broadcasters were known for
radio and television, often local reporters who somehow became
nationally known and loved, like Bas Tubert or Catherine
Saunders. Relda's warm voice and delightful personality made
her the nearest perhaps we have come to a nation's sweetheart
along the lines of Vera Lynn and maybe Cilla Black. There
was another side to Relda. It too was life-threatening and she
wouldn't have it any other way. We talked about that when I
visited her in her rural Horokiwi hideaway up in the hills
above the harbour.*

Relda Familton has gone to the dogs. She still has the
150 sheep and the four horses, but most of her off-
screen time is now taken up with what you might
think the very opposite of her hush-puppy personality, four
sleek and menacing Dobermann pinschers and their nine
puppies.

I took to them like a duck to water, says TV2's personality
reporter.

Actually, she was not doing a lot of onscreen reporting at
the time. Another of the endless shakeups of this restless
medium had cut her back from 20 minutes to a mere five.

She was sitting on what she said was a beaut doco on a clairvoyant who had predicted when Muldoon would tumble next year, 1977. She had dug her determined toes in, was not going to have the doco downsized to a sound-and-vision bite. Relda was fed up with television admin interference, just when it was going so well. The public liked the show, but the public have no say in State television conduct.

Anyway, she said with just a faint frown, a passing little black cloud, anyway, the dogs are what matter now. You see, I am a breeder.

Relda's sweet face was not made for depressing subjects. Her eyes danced away from the television gloom up into her hills. Maybe, she said gaily, she was getting past this media thing.

Telethon was getting a bit much. She could not turn down a worthy cause, but she was stuck in the studio all through the night, doing ditsy things to raise money. Like at 4am she did a handstand. She was piggybacked round the studio. She refused to sing 'How Much Is that Doggy in the Window?' but did take the opportunity to tell viewers the doggies in her front window were $130 each.

But why Dobermanns? Relda shook her fine golden pageboy haircut, tapped her teeth with a comb, smoothed down her green jacket, laughed. Yes, Dobermanns. It was after the seventh burglary. She lived in an isolated place. The police brought her an old Dobermann bitch.

I screamed at them, she says. Told them I didn't want to be eaten before my time.

But being inherently and invariably nice, she took the bitch. Click. She was won over. She became obsessed. Started entering competitions. She went to all the shows, got totally involved, began to win prizes. Now she would like to change their sinister image. They are superb watchdogs. The police had caught a burglar by matching the finger a Dobermann removed.

Ouch. Relda!

Oh, she says airily, I wouldn't sell them to people who wanted them as a gun or a club. I always vet buyers. You can get the occasional problem dog. I had an epileptic one, which had a fit and sank its teeth in my arm. I knew it wanted to kill me. It would probably have torn my throat out if I had pulled back. I clasped it to me and tightened its collar until it gagged and let go.

This is not the peachy, creamy gal we all know and love for her soft touch. Ah, she explains, I'm a country girl, from Hawera, so I know about animals. I had always wanted to get back to the country life, which is why I bought this farm five years ago. It's a way of getting out of public life. I'm not really one for it.

Could've fooled most of us.

Okay, she acknowledges the public speaking comes naturally. She won national oratory prizes when she was at school, won a Field Scholarship to the University of Wisconsin. I came back to radio at a good time, with Bas Tubert, Pete Sinclair, Justin du Fresne.

This was the era when broadcasters were on the standard public service grading and for their modest salary were expected to do anything and everything. She was on the YC classical music, the YA National Radio, the commercial stations, announcing news, having to be dead straight and oh so proper, which was not her bubbly nature. However, she had had the classical training in piano and voice and could do the serious stuff.

What she wanted to do was have the fun guys like Pete and Bas and Justin were having. No girls in commercial radio at that time. She sneaked in the back studio door, working the panel for these three top deejays. She kept doing more and proved good at it, particularly the selling side, so they kept her on.

Outdoor broadcasts were my forté, she says. My best

year was '69, when I got into the local television show *Town and Around*. People still talk about those days, doing goofy things like flying a Vampire jet, getting drunk on milk, jumping into the harbour. Bas did his skating through the Botanic Gardens tulips in his Dracula cloak. People seemed to identify with that show.

Would they still?

Yes, she says, I think they would. But ... things are supposed to be more, well, sophisticated these days.

Those were the days, my friend. On *The Brian Edwards Show* Farmer Brown, the precursor of Fred Dagg, was on the phone about a paddock of dead sheep, calling for Relda. Where is Relda? Relda'll know what to do. That kind of thing, she says with just a faint crack in her honeyed timbre, has gone.

Still, she says, I am an optimist by nature. These 20-minute documentaries I am doing for TV2 – nothing has stretched me as they have. The one where they filmed a childbirth. She had lambed ewes, birthed foals, delivered puppies, but she had never seen a human baby born. She cried her eyes out. Great television. Another big moment was on the Telethon when she interviewed the parents of a blind girl with cerebral palsy. Surely that was worth keeping?

It's a rhetorical question. She knows they don't really want her dewy-eyed stuff; they want hard-nosed interviewers. She was too polite, too much the old school, to go for the jugular. She left that to her dysfunctional Dobermanns and coped when it happened. Telly in any case did not play a big part in her life. In lulls at work or with her parents she enjoyed *Jokers Wild*, Maude and Dick Emery and laughed like a drain at the afternoon soaps, guessing how many seconds the lovers gaze into each other's eyes, so bad it was brilliant.

At home there was no time for telly, with dogs and horses and sheep to feed. Up at 5am, last feed at midnight. If she

82

had one ambition or wish it would be to sing like Kiri. She had an okay voice, we all know that. The passage out, she says, is a bit rough. She was resigned to her lot, had no illusions about widening her talent. She wouldn't mind acting, but nobody wanted to accept her as anybody but herself. A compliment, but for her maybe a bit backhanded.

At present she felt she wasn't really being used much. She was used to full-on broadcasting. Now it seemed like a waste. She was willing, the powers-that-be were not. Such foolish folk. Putting the nation's sweetheart out to grass. She likes the contrast of the farm life, but you can bet she would be in boots and all if she were asked to do her own show. Pity she is considered too soft for today's hard-edged approach. In fact, they are quite wrong. Relda is tough and tender. Imagine how great she would be if they gave her a *Country Calendar* show, or an ambulance chaser show where she talked to people in dire straits, or a chat show where she talked to divas and dancers, performers and prancers, anybody in town. Relda would grace any show, bringing to it her own sympathetic personality, able to cope with the worst tragedies and the best news, death and birth, with that husky voice and sweet manner we now have to settle for hearing more than seeing. When will the programme bosses ever learn?

No matter, says this spunky lass. Want to come see my Dobermanns?

Um, well, I have this deadline, Relda. Maybe ...?

Anytime. Come visit, says this lovely lady whose voice and manner make for a better place. Ask those Telethon kids or the lonely folk who tune into her warm voice making the long nights a little more bearable.

Silverculture Is Seriously and Kiwi Ingeniously Silly

*Unlike L&P, Burton Silver is world famous in the world. Can you think of another Kiwi who does author tours of the States, has serious art analyses of his work in the New York Times and other high falutin' journals in America and Europe, is published in many languages, had a book launched in a San Francisco art gallery, had a Japanese entrepreneur pursuing him for the world ancillary rights to his blockbuster **Why Cats Paint**? You can't, can you? I knew Burton when we were Wellington university students way back in the early 1960s, when he was known for inventing a ski polisher. I played squash with him in London in the early 1970s. Back here I have had some wonderfully naughty and/or bizarre gifts from this spoof artist extraordinaire. Some were on view in the 1994 **Sixty Minutes** tribute to him. Rumours are strong he has even more amazing plans he is about to launch on a willingly credulous world. Back in 1982 we talked about becoming a Kiwi overseas.*

Burton Silver chuckled at the crudity of his first Bogor cartoon strip for the *Listener* back in 1973. The little woodsman who was to run 21 very naughty years in the magazine began sans his classic Kiwi bush singlet. His hard hat looks more like a Quasimodo fungal growth on his back. The happied-out hedgehog looks at this nascent cartooning stage like the squashed result of a highway hit-and-run.

I couldn't see that first effort being accepted overseas, he says with a sceptical eye. Here it is easier to make it. New Zealand is a lovely training ground. It's not nearly so cut-throat, and you can struggle to world class before you hit the world.

Courtesy of Kiwiophile editor Ian Cross, Bogor took no time at all to push the long-running *Punch* cartoon out of the prized possie opposite the editorial. At this time, when Burton and I had just returned from our OE in London and other parts, *Punch* was still considered the acme of all humour, despite its being edited at the time by a business journalist and about as funny as a cup of cold porridge. But we remained under the psychological as well as economic and, worse, cultural tyranny of patronising British patronage.

Bogor the Kiwi woodsman was a precursor of Kiwi cultural change, not long after Murray Ball roared back here and cornered the market on uninhibited violence of the Tom and Jerry and *Beano* comic variety. And Bogor swept up the whimsy market as fast as an Aussie bushfire. He was our version of the famous American cartoon strip *Peanuts*, and only lack of film marketing confidence stopped Bogor following *Peanuts* on to the animated television and movie screens. Burton did write a children's film, 'The Monster's Christmas', set in the weird volcano lands of the central North Island. He could not maintain artistic control so went back to where he could.

His forays into film were restricted to spoof *Country Calendar* items like the radio-controlled dogs, singing fence wires and shampooed sheep. But Bogor was where he honed and refined and evolved his singularly silly perspective on life. The actual development of this weird *weltanschaung* took place abroad. As a student there were only hints of the cheeky chappie to come.

While most of us went straight to London to find a conventional job, Burton stopped off in the Australian desert for several months. There, alone in a strange void, he studied his fantasies and found a sure core to himself. If you can survive that terrifying emptiness, you can survive anything.

It was his rite of passage. Some go to war; Burton tried Christ's approach of a good spell alone in the desert living off the local equivalent of locusts and honey. Bogor was dreamt up in Australia's most remote outback. Bogor's nature and nurture have a lot to do with the way we crave travel almost as much as coming home, and even more to do with how his creator finally found a way of kicking against the pricks of Kiwi conformity.

At school Burton liked pranks more than pass marks, so much so that the headmaster appreciated the joke when Burton confessed to forging a *poor* report for his parents. The headmaster observed it was not the glowing report most forgers would have chosen and then failed him.

That's the way it was then. Those in charge were authoritarian and not known for a sense of humour. Burton's parents tried to impress upon him that life was not a joke. Burton never got the message. To him life is and should be a joke.

Career opportunities were not obvious back then. Like many, I became a teacher because I couldn't think of what else to do. Burton thought he would like to be a journalist. He was told by the editor of the *Evening Post* he would get a three-month trial and then they would tell him if he would make a journalist. While I tried out at the *Listener* and after three months was told I didn't seem to have the right stuff, Burton preferred to go to university and enrol in Asian studies, a trendy new course at the time. He wrote exposés for the university rag *Salient*, whose editor, one Geoffrey Palmer, would skilfully sensationalise. Palmer learned to mute such impulses as he climbed the slippery pole to become PM.

Burton had other plans. He took off for Australia and went on buffalo-hunting expeditions above Darwin. He was a boilermaker on a manganese island. He did a stint as piano accompanist for an Afghani spoon strummer in a desert pub. He did a controversial feature in a local paper on why Darwin had such a high suicide rate.

He came home, spotted a film on short skis, approached cabinetmaker John Bull, who had made Parliament's Cabinet table, and they went into business. People on the ski slopes laughed, looked again, then bought. Burton now knew he was in business.

So he took off again. Those Asian studies became hands on. He was almost killed by a hand grenade in Surabaya and wrote about it for a local paper. He heard stories of fierce Borneo headhunters. He went looking for them. When he found them, he found them friendly but insistent on guests dancing. His version of the haka initially caused much alarm, closely resembling as it did the dance that preceded a headhunt.

On he went to Kashmir, where he advised the high altitude warfare school on ski maintenance.

Back to Australia to teach Aborigine lepers art and English.

Off to Africa with friend Keith, where the old university debate on the meaning of life and testing oneself to find oneself came to a head. So back again to Oz for five months in the desert 400 ks somewhere inland from Darwin, living on fish, wallabies and, it has to be admitted, some packaged food.

He soon realised how much he fantasised. I imagined, he says, friends coming to look at my hut. I hugged trees and they were like people breathing. One day I thought of a little man who lives alone in the forest and lives out his fantasies. The first was making an orchestra out of logs and conducting it.

When the food ran out he came back to Darwin and then home for Christmas. He liked the look of his grandmother's old whare up the back in the trees at Karaka Bay, so he lived there alone with an aquarium of axolotls.

He was hiding out, one could say, above the family home, where generations of Silvers have lived in the old white wooden villa, the Silver baitbox with lock set into the rock across the road below high tide, so the water refreshes the bait.

He encountered the familiar claustrophobia of being back home. You can be overseas indefinitely, he says regretfully, and as long as your letters say you are happy, people don't mind. But once you are back, there is constant pressure from people asking what you do for a living – you are answerable to your friends. I had never thought of being a cartoonist, but I liked making people laugh and I knew I was good at short concepts. I remembered the little fantasy man, perhaps because I was alone in the whare in the bush. I did these drawings and took them in to the *Listener*.

Once he had his woodsman smoking, so to speak, with his snail chariots and hedgehog accompaniment, the fantasies like gazing out over the forest at two mountains with nipples on top, then Burton wanted to extend himself. So he started Ob, about a snake, a stone and a rock, a free play of ideas and concepts that again he traces back to his five months with his own thoughts.

He likes nothing better than talking to children about cartooning and getting them going. He had always fooled around at school because there was no other outlet in those zipped-up days for creativity. He remembers a teacher who said yours not to reason why. Wrong. It depresses him that children are still taught this way. He proposes problems and asks the children to solve them, like a man knocking on the door and the kangaroo answers. Is Mrs Jones in? Yes, she says, popping out of the kangaroo's pouch.

There are as many answers as children. He thinks they are better off learning to solve problems than answering questions like what the tallest mountain is. Develop the ability to manipulate knowledge and make connections and you can leave school and maybe think up jobs like trucking rotten ponga logs from Rotorua to Wellington for decorative fences.

While others have indeed done that one, Burton has moved on to ever more exotic ideas and then proved they could work. When he started giving his friends odd presents for birthdays and anniversaries, we all worried about being unable to reciprocate. I remember Tom Scott and Brian Edwards receiving these beautifully tooled books, which in fact were secret repositories for bottles of alcohol. I got one that played to my owl collection, a book between elaborately carved owls he told me had been his mum's bookends. Out of their new plastic beaks poured, at the touch of a discreet tap, a golden stream of malt whisky, secreted within in a pipette he had acquired from the university chemistry lab. Its stopper was guttapercha pink buttocks. It was all concealed within a sliding top to a book of superbly tooled leather and gold-leaf lettering from Silverculture Press. A work of rare and odd art.

That was but one of many. One year I got chook legs mounted on a macrocarpa log, allegedly a low-flying great owl, another time a collection of feathers with legends retailing owl encounters. Most meticulous was the 'Owlbum' pop-up book of owls and female botties in compromising positions. This may well have been New Zealand's first pop-up book. For sure it was the most popular book for all visitors. Burton borrowed it back during the development of his first international bestseller, *The Naughty Victorian Handbook*, a rude creation of the art of furtling, putting your curled finger or pressed thumb into the cut-out space behind a Victorian lady leaping fences or bending over by the seaside, a spoof on naughtiest Victorian postcard art.

There was no stopping Burton thereafter, with his Kokigami cod paper condoms the Japanese recalled as an ancient art fallen into disuse, his Kama Sutra of Cats, his bird poop on windscreens interpreted as a psychologist would Rorschach inkblots, the best-selling *Why Cats Paint* and its sequel *Dancing with Cats*. In the midst of all this the busy little woodsman turned 21 and was retired with a birthday collection. Burton was too busy overseas developing three-dimensional items that will surely see him on the American version of *60 Minutes*.

And he has also found time to have three children and to turn his old family villa into some kind of Disneyland antique castle full of most wonderful old working objects. Hundreds stroke and murmur and coo over these antiquities when Burton and Melissa have their annual carol singing gathering before a Christmas tree decked out with dozens of tiny beeswax candles in the Dutch barn Burton built beside the sea.

Up in the tree-dense cliff behind him Burton has extended his old whare into a maze of wooden huts for play and work, the two words interchangeable with Burton, and all connected by beautifully finished paths of old sleepers and recycled bricks. When his mate Peter Jackson has finished *Lord of the Rings* in his nearby studios, he might be inspired to film a story in Burton's steep and weird neck of the woods. It could involve that baitbox, Burton's kauri launch or Disneyland house-truck, any number of the strange objects in his house, which in the quiet of night probably start whirring and prancing, the stuffed cat rising to paint, the monkey cranking the barrel organ, the bellows pumped up, out of the art deco lampshades pop ...

Burton definitely has a way with forest products. He had to go overseas to find the way. He had to come home to realise it. Burton, may all your pinecones turn to silver, which they surely will, in ways he can but the rest of us never could ever dream of. Not bad for a lad who claims he can't draw.

Our Greatest Kiwi Sportsman?

A few voices at the selection of the Sportsman of the Century last year suggested Ivan Mauger should have been in for consideration. Ivan who? Well, he was spotted at the ceremony where Peter Snell took the prize, this dark, slender, handsome man in the background. He had been Sportsman of the Year 1977, when he won the fifth of his six world titles, receiving the award from the athlete of that decade, John Walker. No New Zealander, some argue, quite dominated his sport so triumphantly as Mauger did speedway at a time when it was the second biggest spectator sport in the world. The problem was, it was the wrong sport.

Out in the hills above Upper Hutt in February 1973 the sunset was shattered by the unaccustomed snarl of speedway bikes. Although the sport had been dormant here since the 1950s, there were still over 14,000 fans travelling out to this remote spot to sit on the old grey cracked and splintered weatherboard seats of the Te Marua stockcar circuit for the Fourth Speedway Test between Great Britain and New Zealand. The Basin Reserve does not get that many for a cricket test between the two countries.

It looked more like a dusty backcountry rodeo *Country Calendar* might take an amused look at. Yet here were three New Zealand world champions, between them taking half the world championships of the last 20 years, competing in a sport that packed 100,000 fans into Britain's Wembley Stadium for the last world championship, whence live television coverage was beamed to America, Russia, Poland, Sweden, Denmark and most other countries in East and West Europe, for there is no cold war in this hot sport.

The atmosphere and the fans were a clue as to why the

sport is ignored by our media – they come from the other side of the crude wire fence. A sound system that would have your hifi aficionados smirking crackled out that bouncy old song 'Bimbo, Bimbo, where ya goina go-ee-oh?' Scruffy children in bare feet collected armfuls of empty soft-drink bottles, couples in sleeveless T-shirts strolled around, showing off shoulder tatts and dusty leathers. Mini skirts were popular, as were knee-length boots on both sexes. Cowboy hats, perms you no longer see in city streets. Hotdogs and ice-creams, soft drinks and hard drinks. A good-humoured crowd.

'Bimbo' was cut off in mid-question, replaced by throat-clearing and a breezy voice telling everybody we were in for a terrific night's racing. His voice was monstered by a great rumbling and backfiring of heavy motors. Out of the pit-gates hurtled a miniature motorbike ridden by a small boy in helmet and leathers, wobbling as he waved at the yelling, cheering crowd. Behind him rumbled the shake- rattle-and-rolling stockcar procession, speedway stars astride their bonnets like Mad Max gladiators entering their arena.

Gedda a good look, the announced yelled. She's the closest yur'll get to these boys. They'll be burnin' up the track next time ya see them. Here's Nigel Bocock – sorry, Boocock – the English captain ... and here's New Zealand's own world champ ...

The whoops and yodels and shrieks and massed acclamation drowned out his introduction of Ivan Mauger.

Where? Where? a girl cried desperately, jumping up and down, using her friend's shoulder to give her lift.

He's on 16, said her taller friend.

Mauger (pronounced 'major') was sprawled out on 16's bonnet in red, white and blue leathers looking as concerned as Steve McQueen, the long lashes, the lop-sided grin and the dark good looks. Like, say, the fifth Beatle, like any good old cowboy rodeo star, waiting to let his riding do the talking, accepting the female hysteria as part of the show.

Boocock introduced his riders on the fragmented Tannoy system. Mauger stepped up and in a thin but determined voice told the crowd how hard it was to be recognised in New Zealand. Maybe speedway was starting to get recognised at last here. He then introduced Barry Briggs, four times world champ before him, a large, blond man with hunched shoulders, who looked like an Otago hill-country farmer. Then the lean, leathery Ronnie Moore, our first world champ at the sport, retiring this year aged 40.

To the cheers of the crowd the procession retreated and the lights dimmed. The pitbikes fired up, snarling like an approaching swarm of super-wasps. Shrieking menacingly, the bikes reared towards the flimsy starting tape, barely constrained by their anonymous riders swathed in helmets, goggles and face masks.

As the starting gate whipped up, the bikes rose like drag racers, one shooting into the lead, bending through the first corner at 100 kilometres per hour, showering an arc of dirt and stones on the three bikes close behind, the noise ear-splitting, the smell of something like aviation fuel heavy in the air. I couldn't believe what the photographer was doing, heading straight for the far corner as the bikes wound up down the back straight, getting up to 150 kph, broadsiding because they have no brakes round the bend, the photographer disappearing completely behind a hail-wave of gravel. I watched horrified at the snarling cluster of riders, the front wheels held at right angles, left legs propped out, dragging the ground on the steel toecaps, guiding the riders at a few degrees off horizontal, defying gravity and all rational behaviour, particularly for the photographer staring down the lens a metre from these black knights charging.

Remarkably, I saw Bill Beavis still upright as the bikes flashed past. He must have copped a faceful of dirt and stones, but he had a photo to get, and photographers are by nature foolhardy. Relieved, I tried to make out what was happening as the bikes were approaching up the home straight with apocalyptic sound and fury, a British flag on the chest of the rider overtaking, before the dip into the next corner saw the Kiwi flag rider cut through on an impossible right-angle slide and shriek away up the back straight.

Four times in one minute these riders belted round the circuit. By this time the Kiwi well clear at the chequered flag. As he coasted to a stop, the applause was peppered with girlish shrieks as the announcer told us Mauger had taken the first race.

Briggs won the second heat; Moore was leading the third when he developed mechanical failure. Mauger lead from the start in all his six heats, his winning margin growing with each race as he ground down the opposition with inexorable, chanceless, consummate, almost monotonous skill. New Zealand won the test to square the series two nil. What surprised me was the Brits had won two tests. Briggs and Moore are still among the best in the world; Mauger is the best, many say the best of all time. At this stage he has 10 world championship medals and is a household name to millions in Eastern as well as Western Europe and America. The same fans would not have heard of the All Blacks.

Off the circuit Mauger sports floral shirts, gold bracelets, high-heeled shoes, and his dark good looks have made him a pin-up. In Britain he has been a regular television panellist alongside the likes of boxer Henry Cooper, the only person to knock down Muhammad Ali, and English World Cup-winning soccer captain Bobby Moore. Although speedway is not televised much in Britain, it does get 100,000 fans a week, second only to soccer, enough for Mauger to have been voted third as their Sportsman of the Year and fourth three times in four years for the title of Television Personality of the Year, a programme with 20 million viewers. I was there as a journalist and recall the rumours that he was actually voted by viewers higher than fourth, but these oiky lower class motorbike riders have to be kept in their place. No question he is doing well, with advertising contracts for oil and leathers, helmets and chains, chewing gum and clothes. He has property investments, drives a white Mercedes.

And every year over the last decade he comes back here, often alone, never any publicity, to promote New Zealand speedway. After this meet, the Brits went back home and Ivan went to Wanganui, to race, then Palmerston North two days later, Gisborne the next day, Napier the day after, Christchurch for the weekend meet, Hamilton on the Sunday, and Tuesday off to Daytona, Florida.

Ivan looked super cool in his floral shirt when I sat down for a chat later. He was not cool about the indifference, even hostility to him here, more like puzzled. In LA or Sydney, he says, wherever else, they give me a car. Here I borrow my mum's. I guess they never do rate the home lad.

There is obviously a very tough streak in him. There'd have to be to dominate this sport, most of whose practitioners are riding with broken bones in hands and fingers, if not ribs, or ones scarcely knitted. Ivan goes the extra yards beyond his colleagues not only in his servicing of his bikes but in his single-minded determination to fan the flames of the sport here. He acknowledges speedway is not the in-thing, not since the 1950s. Now people have cars. There are still plenty who like to ride bikes, just nobody wanting to watch any more. He guesses it could be the media publicity about Hell's Angels and other bikie hooligans puts people off, parents steering their kids away from these louts. He thinks there may be at last a swing away from this, given that speedway in recent times at

Western Springs in Auckland, at Templeton in Christchurch, has trebled to five-figure marks.

He wants to see more bums on those splintered seats. That is why he does not take days off to go to the beach. He does the appearances in the provinces, trying to get the crowds back.

Mauger is the third generation link out of Christchurch, third world champ behind Moore in the 1950s, Briggs in the 1960s. Ronnie Moore, he says, was his childhood idol. Champions attract more champions.

But how come we have so many world champions? He reckons it is something in the Kiwi temperament. We've got a passive nature, he says, which is good under pressure. Look at Snell and Halberg, or the grand prix drivers Hulme, McLaren and Amon. In speedway you get a tremendous amount of pressure. I watched the Dane Ole Olsen ride spectacularly to pass riders. I reckon he should have settled for second, but he tried to pass the leader and fell off. To me that means he's not good enough, even though he won the next four races.

Ivan of course was the leader. While Olsen has been in tears at what he considered bad luck, Ivan accepted the breaks. He was leading the world champs in 1967 until he was knocked off his bike and lost by one point. He won the next three world champs, the first man to do so. He did it by being focused. He talks of being booed at beating British riders there. It does not concern him. Winning does. He does not smile and wave like other riders – well, not much.

While others might get caught up in the gut-churning, acrid, adrenalin-charging excitement of the sport, Ivan stays majorly calm. He is there to win, not to please. He is rated the best starter in the sport, but losing rivals call him a gate-jumper. He times his run like a good yachtsman, so he is moving when the start line is crossed. I remember the spectacular sight at a Wimbledon meet of a rival so anxious to pip Ivan at the start, he went with the starting gate up in the air and down very hard, and out. I don't know what injury he sustained that time, but one rider told me of a broken arm and leg and innumerable bruises, of riding with a broken finger, once one-eyed after a stone sliced through his goggles. At least one rider is killed each year, not a high average given the pile-ups you are pretty well guaranteed to see each meet, riders running over and into each other at over 100 kph. Even the sign at the entrance to Wimbledon suggests it is not just the riders who should be wary. 'You attend at your own risk,' it says. The wire barrier may be high, but sometimes the bikes do get over the safety barrier.

None of this is anything other than par for the course. Maybe that is why Ivan concentrates on getting out of the gate first, ahead of trouble. Ivan won that race where the driver hit the gate, yet it was another rider, a youngster on the way up, who had his helmet off and shaking out his long blond locks, impressing the girls. Later the speedway manager told me that on trips to Paris, your ruddy Kiwi riders make me wait in line when they pick up the girls, no respect for their bosses and betters.

Mauger does not bother with that side of things. I have seen a photo of Ivan with the bosomy starlet Sabrina craning forward to kiss him, Ivan not meeting her halfway. He is a married man. He is there to win, not wave. He is a meticulous mechanic, a clinically cool rider, and off his stage a laconic Kiwi. He is probably the best rider this raw sport has seen. He might be the best sportsman we have produced.

The First Dinkum Kiwi Writer

*John A. Lee lived in the shadow of the intemperate pamphlet he wrote attacking Labour leader and Prime Minister Michael Joseph Savage. It got him expelled from the Labour Party in 1940, and he spent the rest of his long life in the socialist wilderness. If not for that, New Zealand may have been denied the wonderfully droll stories he concocted about the tramp Shiner Slattery, who began the tradition continued by Barry Crump and those two Taranaki writers Ronald Hugh Morrieson and Frank S. Anthony with his Gus Tomlins of the mythological Kiwi con-artist and a confident post-colonial sense of good feeling about being Kiwis. Lee himself was never so benign, as inflamed a writer as Alan Duff, a passionate political orator Muldoon learned at the feet of. Before he shot himself in both left feet, Lee wrote the autobiographical novel of his poor Dunedin childhood **Children of the Poor**. When Ian Cross was sending me off to interview the venerable Lee, he said that when his novel **The God Boy** came out he got a telegram from Lee congratulating him on a real New Zealand novel. Cross replied: You wrote the first New Zealand novel.*

John Alfred Alexander Lee opened the front door of his modest Auckland suburban home. The broad Irish potato face, a nose shining in the darkness of the dark and modest state house kind of hallway, a searching assessment of my brother and I.

McGill and McGill, you say, he said bluntly. Sounds like a firm of solicitors. Still, if young Cross sent you, you'd better come in. Good writer.

He turned and we followed his big, bent-over frame. You've got till the Melbourne Cup starts, he growled over his shoulder, to talk about Sir Ernest Booze.

The reference was to his new book, the putative reason for the interview, to let him paraphrase another hatchet job, *For Mine is the Kingdom*.

Lee took the old easy chair, positioned himself with the one hand the size of a road-driller's. He accepted the half-glass of sweet sherry from his wife.

First Cup I've witnessed, he boomed. And, mark you, I'm 84 come last month.

He looked pretty hale on it, the hair iron grey, like the political will, unbent, unbowed, the spirit doing better than the body, our oldest and still our most irreverent statesman, waving the stump of his left arm, a World War One wound, ready to pour forth the intoxicating views in his latest book on the country's biggest brewer.

Ernest Davis had five millions and 200 hotels, said Lee, an aggregate not seen before or since. He lived when there was scope for the supreme racketeer, before private concerns went public and corporate, when The Trade dominated politicians and Ernest dominated The Trade. He became sanctified as Mayor of Auckland and leader of the winning racehorse list for years, gave the Queen Mother a racehorse and got a knighthood.

Lee talks with the cold contempt of an IRA splinter group zealot. One reviewer, he said with harsh amusement in his voice, accused me of being holier than thou. He should know that nobody has written more about himself than me, about going to an industrial school and being whipped often, being in jail at 21, going to Australia with another man's wife, and being the brunt of malicious lies that had me expelled from the Labour Party, for which I harbour no bitterness, for it liberated me from the dilemma I always had of whether to be writing or politiking.

There was nothing left but to write for the next four decades in the wilderness, yet, Lee confirms, he remained a political figure. Evidence, if needed, is the three publishers who rejected his book on Sir Ernest Booze. The publisher who accepted is, not surprisingly, the principal protest publisher in the country, Alister Taylor, as keen to challenge the system as Lee ever did with the likes of the Establishment-condemned *Little Red Schoolbook*. Hard to know why Lee didn't cut to the chase and go to Alister first up.

There's more to come, Lee vows. I told Keith Holyoake the other day I'd be remembered 100 years after him – for the diaries I'm writing now. Lee leans back, to clear the tubes. You see, he booms, they'll still be execrating me then. The old iconoclast lets go with a roar of triumphant laughter. Nobody ever kept John A. Lee down.

He does need to get his breath back, sitting there in his old brown suit, red flannel roadman's singlet under the grey shirt. Lee dismissively calls himself decrepit. It won't stop his mission. The eyes burn, banked up by old political fires. There's still work to do. This is his 13th book, but he has seven more planned. He tends the tomatoes out the back of his Mount Albert home, but he is not just settling for the old-age pension and social security his missionary party had so much to do with advancing, in particular the state housing he was Labour's point man for. Never mind the dignified old age he espoused as a young man, he has plans. The corner of his street pays homage to him, recently named John A. Lee corner. So it should.

Lee has always been a fighter. He survived his childhood with his fighting instinct. Private Lee won a DCM in the war after taking a machinegun post on his own. The war took his left arm. He has never stopped fighting the good fight, though he has not had many awards between the war and the corner – unless you count book sales. *Children of the Poor* sells 3000 a year, up to 53,000, is known internationally, was praised by American novelist Upton

103

Sinclair as one of the most human documents he had ever read, and by George Bernard Shaw with sub-Shavian wit as a whopper! Lee's engaging tramp-on-the-scam Shiner stories are currently being filmed for television, so soon publicans all over the country will have to endure the famous Shiner trick of getting a free meal out of them.

The author says he prefers to write fact now, laced with 'permissible' fiction. He says there is a lack of personal accounts of the Prohibition/Trade conflict, before the Depression shifted the issue from beer and water to bread and butter. For him Davis was the shadowy Rasputin behind political life at a time when The Trade was fighting to survive, its one-and-a-quarter percent levy aptly termed the Slush Fund, used to unlock Prohibition. It succeeded, he claims, for the majority voted dry, but politicians voided the mandate.

I worked in a Davis hotel as a kid, he says. I saw who came to dinner: the likes of Sir Joseph Ward, Sir Gordon Coates and Micky Savage – that barrel washer for Davis.

There is the unyielding contempt for Michael Joseph Savage, Labour's first prime minister, whom Lee served very directly as his Parliamentary Under-Secretary. The old Lee is bitter only in the hearty, hoppy sense of a good beer, but he is as cold as Aussie draught with his class-conscious rage, coldest when identifying a traitor to his working class.

When I became MP for Auckland East, he continues, Davis had the brewery there and four-fifths of the hotels. He contributed to my campaign funds. Later he paid to have me expelled from the Party. Likewise, he was the power behind ousting Arnold Nordmeyer and installing Norman Kirk. And he was the paymaster for trade union leader Fintan Patrick Walsh.

Ernest's hotels, Lee continues, his voice hardening, if that is possible, they were held together with paint and profit. He did see the need to hand over shares to the public, and now the breweries run more decent establishments. Today it is the Trusts that pour the profits into making the drinking troughs wider, deeper and cheaper. Nobody envisioned that when the Trusts began that they would become booze barns, bending nothing back to the community. At least the breweries return some money to shareholders.

Lee is up on his soapbox, building up a head of steam, his voice deepening, resonating, finally thundering out against Trusts profiteering out of control from the money injected by wild-drinking 18-year-olds. There could, he warns, be a resurgence of the Temperance Movement. The average mother and the average father, they tell me they fear their children coming home from school filled up with booze! I'm no puritan ... but I tell you, I can see young girls dropping their defences and getting into trouble. If a barman can't tell 18 from 20, how can he be expected to tell a 16-year-old from an 18-year-old?

We don't breed 'em like Lee any more. So, does he rate any of the current crop?

Beetham has presence, but he reads his speech! Labour, they look like a bunch of 'civil' servants! Muldoon was the only man with the voice for the course. You know, Muldoon was at all my soapbox speeches in Albert Park, in short pants. He knew what the others didn't realise, that you had to get match fit. I trained by singing an hour a day with my mouth closed.

Is there a touch of the Shiner Slattery bulldust in that? No matter, in his political heyday Lee was magic. He retains the biggest Parliamentary majority ever. He is match fit, still in print. His prophecies of Prohibition may seem fanciful, but just you wait, he shouts, until you catch sight of a few thousand teenage alcoholics.

Much more of this fire and brimstone and one might be signing the pledge. Thankfully the Melbourne Cup was about to start. Race books, Lee once told the Indecent

Publications folk, are the literature most likely to corrupt the young. In his old age Lee is incorruptible. He has outlasted all his foes. Yet there remains work to do, to create the juvenile protections he never had as a youth. In this he is as evergreen as a clump of bright green moss in a grey Kerry bog. That I would drink to, as indeed we did when we had driven off and stopped to wet our very dry whistles at the next booze barn.

The Planting of Kiwi Preservation

In the mid-1950s Old St Paul's Anglican cathedral was to be replaced by a new St Paul's. The cathedral committee dismissed the little old wooden Gothic church as a mere curiosity and prepared to pull it down. They did not reckon on a small band of their parishioners objecting. Prominent among them was Betty Plant, who was ready to camp in the old church, if that was required. She had not been captain of the Cathedral Corps of Girl Guides for nothing. She got help in high places in what became the first big fight to save New Zealand's fledgling heritage, in the process of which the New Zealand Historic Places Trust was formed.

Old St Paul's is a church for all sects and all seasons. I was married there in a Catholic service, my daughter was baptised there, and I have been to many funerals there. I am one of the tens of thousands of visitors who keep coming back every year to this glorious little wooden church to sit on kauri pews with their feet on gleaming matai floors. I cast my eyes heavenwards past the great brass eagle lectern and the flower-bedecked altar to those soaring arcs of Gothic wood, willingly trapped in this sacred ribcage, wherein Bach and Handel play softly and holy light radiates through the rich stained-glass windows to cast God's grace upon all who enter. Here, surely, is a place where the weary traveller may find rest, a deconsecrated church where all faiths and sects may worship, a concert chamber nonpareil for the best of classical music making. Thanks be to Betty Plant.

People come in here, says Miss Plant, curator of Old St Paul's, looking for peace. Recently a man came in so distraught I thought I should send him across the road to the Samaritans at the Cathedral. He stayed 25 minutes. He came back 10 days later and told me of the repose he found here.

Every visitor to Old St Paul's over many years has had some contact with Miss Plant. She plays the music. She has arranged the flowers. She has polished every plank and the myriad brass plaques from pulpit to porch, everything once a week. She was not amused by the raucous remark of an Australian visitor, exclaiming, 'Why, there's no dust!'

I am the labourer, says Miss Plant. I love Old St Paul's, and if you are doing something you love, it's no effort. The Almighty gives me the time, the roller skates and the energy.

Miss Plant has earned help from on high for her lifelong devotion to this church. Her parents came out from England and were married here. She became captain of the Cathedral Corps of the Girl Guides when it was still the Anglican Cathedral, and it was then she first laboured in the Lord's vineyard to enhance the warm brown splendour of the place.

And then the Lord tested her sorely. She says she is a died-in-the-wool Anglican, but those years in the 1950s fighting the Anglican authorities who would destroy her church, why, she still feels the distress of that time. It was necessary for her to denounce this heretical proposal by her own priests and luminaries, and she a mere humble servant on her knees in prayer and with polishing rag. The Cathedral Committee loftily offered to placate their agitated parishioner protest by suggesting some of the silly old building could be incorporated in a corner of the new. No thank you, said the lemon-lipped protesters. The committee had better and more important things to do raising money for the new cathedral. They washed their hands of the old dump, offering it to the government.

This could have been tantamount to offering an old synagogue to a Roman emperor. However, the small band calling themselves Friends of Old St Paul's had started to attract big players on their team. Dr J.C. Beaglehole had finished his biography of Captain Cook and saw a new task, saving the first remnants of the country Cook had discovered. He stood up in lay pulpits and penned for the *Listener*, then the intellectual and moral voice of the country, rhetoric worthy of the Old Thunderer, *The Times*. We are burning our history, the professor denounced, with the same blind stupidity we burned our forests. Old St Paul's woods would never be used again to this extent and with this feeling, for the feeling has gone, like the forests. It is the community's right to have this beautiful building preserved.

In 1958 further high help came from an unexpected quarter, the visiting architectural historian Nikolaus Pevsner. Even in England, he said, Old St Paul's would be regarded as an outstanding example of the mid-Victorian period. It was a bit of a backhanded compliment and scarcely went very far. He could have said that it was in fact New Zealand's unique contribution to world architecture, wooden Gothic, call it Colonial Gothic if you want a tag for wood masquerading as stone, native New Zealand woods aping British and European stone edifices. And Old St Paul's is the masterpiece of the man who invented this Kiwi colonial adaptation of Old World design.

Brits last century had been more forthcoming. Bishop Selwyn sent his architect, the Reverend Frederick Thatcher, to Wellington, assuring the local Bishop Graham that Thatcher 'will be a treasure to you'. Thatcher proved to be a treasure to all of us with this design of Old St Paul's, using matai, totara, kauri and rimu in a way nobody has bettered, if even come near. He was also its first minister, though ill health forced his resignation before he saw his masterpiece completed.

Betty Plant would much rather talk about him than those who would destroy his masterpiece. She is a truly inspired guide to this sanctuary. If you think a lady with carefully tended silver-white hair and sensible clothes is not going to be interesting, then you have missed the gleam in the eyes behind those thick black librarian glasses. This is her library, and she has an encyclopaedic knowledge of all its ways.

She will direct you to a detail, such as the elaborate carving on a prayer desk. Look at the mouse, she advises. The dragon. The gargoyle. Hector Bolitho gave us that. Came from old Coventry Cathedral. See those trefoils.

Trefoils?

Three-cornered sculpture, symbolic of the Trinity. The trefoil is everywhere, on pews, windows, columns. The reason? This church was dedicated on Trinity Sunday, June 6, 1866.

She concedes it is difficult to see all the detailing. But that is as it should be. She has resisted requests for more light. The dim, dark light of religion, she explains. Aids meditation. Enriches the woods.

She crouches among the pews to point out a particularly rich matai grain. Maybe too beautiful to be on the floor. We get, she says, a lot of admirers of woods here, architects and builders, even Australians. She saw a big Australian studying the extravagant interlocking of crossbeams, like the inside of an upside sailing ship under construction. She asked him was he a builder, and he was. She told him the entire church was built of wood, even unto the nails. He paused a full 10 seconds, then looked down on this sensibly dressed dame and said, 'This church is put together with love.'

Its curator partakes of the mysterious communion with her church. You look happily married, one visitor told her. No, she said, she was not married, but she did love this church. The visitor told her he was a psychiatrist.

See those hooks, she says, perhaps changing the subject. They were for top hat and handbag. Hooks at either end of the pew, the children between parents. That metal square was where the new rental was entered. Those handles, they are for hearing aids. Do you know why the south-side porch is over there? Lord Glasgow, the Governor General, paid 10 pounds to have the southerly draught removed from his back. An American coveted this handle here, wanted to purchase it. I told him two million wouldn't buy it.

She has a story about the bishop's crozier, the dean's stall, the baptistry windows. Her job is truly a labour of love. She makes use of the anecdotes of visitors to express her feeling. She told an American the government bought the church and gave it to the people of New Zealand. No, said the American, they gave it to the world.

She goes further. You could travel the world, she says, and not see a finer church. This church is warm, welcoming, intimate, and it has lived, which stone never has.

People closely associated with the church live on in its fine brass plaques. The one of Dean Davis, its first dean, reads: 'Than Whom No Man Was More at Home in This House of God.'

Better than that, Miss Betty Plant: 'Than Whom No Person IS More at Home in This House of God.'

A Prescription from the Irish Kiwi Chat Doctor

*Brian Edwards has been talking to and at us most of our Kiwi television lives. His most recent incarnation was as the mellow dispenser of the most popular radio Kiwi cultural fix, his National Radio Saturday 'Top o' the Morning' show. That ended with a contract renewal he could only refuse. Brian has suffered more than most broadcasters from the decision makers, but this may be the first time there was a suggestion he was not in step with his audience. He electrified our current affairs screens as our version of David Frost, roasting politicians and even resolving disputes on screen. He took the consumer complaint programme **Fair Go** to the top ratings it still enjoys. He did numbers of chat shows, and he and his wife Judy Callingham discovered a reconnection of missing persons TV series that was not renewed. People like our present prime minister have been happy to employ Brian to teach them how to get in media touch with the nation. Brian will bounce back somewhere. Meantime, here is his turn to answer questions, back in 1976.*

D r Brian Finbar Myram Edwards sat hunched over the latest newspaper criticisms of his chat show. Dressed in a black jersey, unshaven, a bit messy, the acerbic interviewer was holed up in his Avalon Studios eyrie high above the bland Hutt Valley. He looked tired, more the target than the bird of prey we have all come to know and ... ah, watch.

Just looking at the gutter filth for a minute, he said, peering savagely over his tinted glasses and the top of a plastic pot plant.

An air of lassitude hung over the Edwards office. In one

corner Muldoon's least favourite interviewer, Simon Walker, munched a filled roll and engaged in desultory conversation with researcher Mary Strang. Gloomily, Dr Edwards said he was reading all the crits. He confessed to being sensitive about reviews. They tended to upset him, even if there was one bad one and the other nine were nice. He found it frustrating he was not supposed to reply to criticisms, specially where the facts were wrong. Often he wrote a reply anyway, then ripped it up. A kind of self-therapy perhaps.

Critics, he confided, never influenced his own viewing. If he liked a current affairs programme, he cared not a fig what was printed about it. He watched everything. Yes, you could say he was addicted. Being a house-husband helped. The set went on for *Playschool* and stayed on until 10.30 at night. He had this need to be entertained, for passive escapism. He didn't like books. Maybe he stuffed too many down his intellectual gullet getting his doctorate. Now he prescribed television.

It's tremendously relaxing, he said, beginning to warm and come back on to his more familiar challenging style. It drains the anxieties, he adds.

Is he waiting for my surprised reaction? Is this a pose? One has always sensed how much he likes shocking people's expectations, particularly of himself. A kind of iconoclast, the good doctor. Maybe he detected the puritan disapproval of television among our educated classes. So, indulge him. What did he like?

A thin smile of pure anticipation. *Kojak*, he says. Definitely detectable behind the tinted glass is the beady gleam of a revived bird of prey.

I had watched enough of Brian's shows to know what to do. I waited.

I watch more TV2, he said provocatively.

I wait.

Because, he says, they have more escapist drama.

114

Anything else?

He grabs a *Listener*. Humour is highest on his list. Dave Allen, the Irish stand-up comic, is a favourite, and indeed Brian can give him a run for his jokey money. Les Dawson, the large Northern English spinner of surreal stories. And the cheerily competitive *Jokers Wild*.

I wait as he flicks about the programme pages. Yes, he says, high adventure and human-interest dramas like *South Riding*.

The smile is back, a scalpel smile. I'm not fond of current affairs, he says. I watch them out of a sense of obligation, except for *Man Alive*, the human-interest kind of documentary. The one about bad neighbours – that was fantastic. I'm more interested in what is happening over the fence than in Uganda.

Any particular reason?

The scalpel cut across his pursed lips. I relate it to my own skills, which are intuitive and perceptual. Programmes that cater for this I like. Even bad programmes.

He is master of the timing of his pause, another sharp smirk. Absolutely fascinating, he says with controlled relish, like *Opportunity Knocks* and its local equivalent.

Okay. He has identified the bottom of the television barrel. What else did he do off camera?

Basically I am a passive person, he confides, hands meeting across his chest like a defrocked priest at peace with his own conscience. It's too much effort, he continues, to go to the cinema, to listen to radio. Not enough adrenalin in radio to excite him. I need, he says, one hand uncurling for emphasis, very high stimulation. I am a very visual person. Barry Crump summed it up in a recent interview he did with the good, keen man. Crump said he was not interested in going anywhere or meeting anyone. Edwards ditto.

But you are always meeting ...?

115

He has caught me. I have been hooked like an unwary mouse. This is no lay confessor; that hand has uncurled into a claw. It has drawn blood.

I am never ... he says, withdrawing his hands, one going behind his ear, some kind of preening gesture?

I wait.

... interested in meeting the guest before the programme. In 1970 I met Canadian Prime Minister Pierre Trudeau beforehand and physically could not string a sentence together. Once I got the cue sign, I was self-confident, outgoing, articulate, abrasive.

If you tend to be threatened by emotional relationships, he says generously, the studio offers a safe, sterile, public relationship. I know many broadcasters who have difficulties in their personal lives. At present I am working on my relationships to people, trying to be more open, less cold.

This time I wait, gob-smacked. The fierce television doctor threatened by people. This is not possible. Is it?

I know it will destroy my career, he continues in encounter group vein. Another ex-television celebrity told me that. I don't mind. I'm more interested in personal relationships than television. I get no joy from being enormously successful. It's like being the fastest gun in the West. Somebody is always gunning for you. You can't be real and be successful on television. You don't think David Frost is real ...?

Well, no. I met him once, when I was sitting in on a Rolling Stones rehearsal with Mick Jagger getting more and more lewd. Frost rushed in, said breathlessly, 'Wonderful, Michael, super, terrific,' and was out the studio door again without even looking. Ooops. I am not here to talk about me. Big mistake.

Brian is patiently waiting for me to finish my reminiscence, like a cat might wait for a naive mouse to finish cleaning its whiskers, before the pounce.

I am trying, he continued when I discontinued, to improve my value system. I feel less interest in projecting an image. I am reading a bit, *The Dice Man*, where you run your life by a random throw of the dice. We have all these cells or images, but most never get the chance to get out. We all wear masks, tending to provide the one people expect. Now I'm trying to change. My wife is pleased.

Self-analysis? For sure, this was not what I expected from our most daunting interviewer. But I guess that's my problem. Dr Brian seems to be getting crows-feet around the eyes, so maybe he really is smiling about a better private life. Maybe I was misreading the smile. Is it possible this eagle of an interviewer is mellowing out? Or was he underneath always like this? Time to check out his past.

What was your childhood like?

I was a Belfast boy, he says. But I used to travel on the youth hostel circuit round Southern Ireland. They are not logical and industrious like us Northern Irishmen, the original Scots. They have the Celtic twilight of superstition, little people and magic, a psychic sixth sense you can see in Edna O'Brien's novels. I dared to say in a 1969 television documentary that Ireland and Ulster were divided by hatred and bigotry instilled in children from the cradle to the grave. My life was threatened; I required police protection.

Brian had left in 1965 to get away from the incessant religious sectarianism. It came too close to home when he got engaged to a Catholic girl and his mother attempted suicide. She was convinced the Catholics would not practise birth control so they could eventually spawn enough to take over. Brian thinks the Irish are fine once they get out of Ireland. He now considers himself a New Zealander.

So do we, even though he has never lost that lovely soft Irish accent. It has allowed him to get away with the hard questions that, say, young Public School Pom Simon Walker has been hammered for. Brian left a hard country and

117

brought a hard style with him. Maybe he is changing again, leaving the hard questions behind in favour of something teetering on the brink of mellowing out? What prescription will Kiwis get next from this bold, maybe born-again media doctor?

The Pom Who Put the Laugh in the Public Kiwi Persona

*When I was flatting with Roger Hall in 1964, we watched Richard Briers in the comedy series **Marriage Lines** on this new phenomenon, television. Roger said his ambition was to have Briers perform his comedy in the West End of London. We Kiwi flatmates thought that a hoot, about as likely as the Archbishop of Canterbury dropping in to join us for shoulder chops and our student version of sauerkraut, cabbage soused in DYC malt vinegar. Five years later I was working for a British television magazine, interviewing Briers and Co on a regular basis. Five years on I was back here in time to catch Roger about to realise his dream of Briers playing in his play in the West End and winning best West End play for **Middle Age Spread**. In 1976 Roger was on the cusp of becoming New Zealand's most successful playwright.*

Roger Hall is sitting at his desk in the old wooden Government Buildings' annexe, a cubbyhole of many coats of public-service cream over the match-lining, the view out the window of a similar cubbyhole a few metres away. It is not easy to find. The venerably creaky old building once housed the entire corpus of MPs and all their public servants. This Nissen hut add-on has some curious kind of brown linoleumed ramp and doors that bump into each other and sandwich the passerby. This is not a user-friendly environment; this is where School Publications have been squeezed, Roger trapped among piles of paper lying like yellowing, curling, teetering stalagmite stacks all around his desk. There is another chair, but moving the papers off it is a threat to the entire dodgy edifice of the editor of one of the Education Department's magazines.

Would you like a cuppa? asks this so-polite Pom as he extends a long arm unfolding in cantilever fashion over his fragile environment.

If it's not too much trouble, I respond, having learned from five years in London some of the same mild-mannered means of meeting all situations. No matter the chaos threatening, always present a stiff upper lip.

With ritualised skill Roger manoeuvres us out the door and around to the califont, pronging it to whistle up boiling water. An old aluminium teapot, the half-empty pint of milk minus its foil skullcap, the chipped cup full of Chelsea, white cups not quite as thick as the old Railway cups but reassuringly Kiwi-public-service plain. Roger is tidy in his three-piece suit, hair parted strictly down the side, the lean, attentive face of a model civil servant who has just written a comedy about our public service, which seems unlikely. Nobody had ever suggested all those faceless 60,000 servants in Wellington were anything to laugh about. At nine they arrive on the trains or the buses, grey columns entering downtown offices with metronomic regularity; at five they leave in ant-like procession for the railway station. Surely not a lot of laughs there. But, the new actors' coop Circa Theatre, breakaway from the established Downstage Theatre, is getting its first big numbers for Roger's public service comedy *Glide Time*, so somehow Roger has mined a comedy vein out of the public service rubble during his decade beavering away as a teacher and now education editor.

Back in his dangerously tilted government-issue swivel chair, he doesn't look as crushed as one might expect, but then under his somewhat lugubrious demeanour there always was an antic streak. As students we had played a most vigorous game of hall soccer, no play on his name, just an all-in brawl, scoring goals through our respective bedroom doors with a rolled-up ball of paper. And all the while he would be doing his imitations of the huskier actors like old Roger Livesey or George C. Scott, making me laugh, allowing him to score again. Then over the over-grilled shoulder chops he would divert us with his hilarious imitations of pompous Kiwi Keith Holyoake, a turn he did sometimes in the student revues he wrote and produced with Steve Whitehouse.

It's my first play for the stage, he says cautiously over the rim of his white cup.

A friend told him it would make an ideal sitcom for television. Well, Roger has been down that path, in 1974 writing the first Kiwi telly sitcom *Buck House*, which the television powers-that-are lost their nerve with and canned too soon. Roger is mildly indignant, probably because he religiously maintains a mild persona. He should be and may be furious about its not being given the fair go all new series need, but his solution is to go on to the next thing. It seems that Kiwi administrators have no confidence that New Zealand can produce its own comedy.

Hall soldiered on, a man of stubborn ambition. He had come out here aged 19 for a better life than North London offered. I had met his parents there and thought it wasn't a bad life. His father was secretary of the Charles Lamb Society and as such knew my father's best friend Professor John Reid of Auckland University. I could see where Roger got his sense of humour – his father came across as the classic, anonymous, middle-class, staid accountant, but he was a very funny man. I was reminded of Pooter in *Diary of a Nobody*, the way the English can manufacture humour out of the mildest material. So maybe Roger had a chance with this theatre play after all.

Roger had written a television play that seemed more likely, about snooker players on the West Coast, from a short story about the black ball hovering on the edge of the hole. He conceded people seemed to remember it, but there is no skiting from Roger. He is a careful man. He had just sold it to radio, so he couldn't really discuss it. Yes, it had been nominated for best script. Yes, it was up against another of his television efforts, about the reading of a will. And he had done a third about an unmarried couple hiring a bach for the weekend. That had copped flak from middle New Zealand, cries to the editor of 'filth!'

Come to that, there were objections to his *Buck House* scenario featuring a mixed flat, yet nobody protested about the similar situation in the English comedy *Man About the House*. Anyway, he shrugs, it never quite came off. He thought having an extra channel now might ease the intense Ma Grundy scrutiny of everything homegrown on telly, for people could now switch over if they didn't like something.

Were you a casualty of that one-channel phase?

Another shrug. For two years he had not been required much. He had done two scripts for the telly soap *Close to Home*, but they were rewritten, to put it mildly, he mildly observes.

Anyway, he got heartily sick of not hearing people laugh at his efforts. He had got used to laughs aplenty in his university revues. He had written 25 revues, graduating down the hill from university to Downstage Theatre, where the likes of the young John Clarke, Ginette McDonald and Paul Holmes were also trying for laughs. Roger had now gone back to this milieu because he wanted to know which lines made people laugh, something you never knew on television.

You did on American television, he continued, because they had audiences, the likes of *The Mary Tyler Moore Show* and *Mash*. It could go too far, says this inherently cautious Englishman. The likes of *Maude* and *All in the Family* were killed by over-applause. In *The Odd Couple* the other night Tony Randall did a minor gymnastic feat and the audience burst into clapping. They were applauding the actor, not the character, Roger says disapprovingly. That was too intrusive.

He had become, he admits, 'a bit disenchanted' with television writing because the writer was never consulted. He provided the material, but he seemed to be bottom of the production barrel. And the pickings were lean; apart from *Close to Home* just a few scripts for *The Brian Edwards Show*.

For him the only real pleasure in writing was creating your own characters, not writing about those made up by somebody else. *Close to Home* was like writing a crossword puzzle.

Last year Roger scored a Queen Elizabeth II Arts Council scholarship to tour Britain and America, studying television and writing. He spent a day with John Finch, who wrote about 400 episodes of *Coronation Street* before creating *Family at War* and then *Sam*, the biggest work for television written by one person. Finch told him he would never work with or be a script editor again because it was insulting to a writer's work. Roger clearly was impressed by the epic possibilities. If Finch could do it, why not him?

Characters are what Roger looks for on television. The best seem to come from America at present. His favourite is Charlton the doorman in *Rhoda*, somebody you never see, yet he has become a living character. He likes Rhoda's sister Brenda too, a loser. And *Barney Miller* is crammed with characters, like the Chinaman who must have the most battered face on the box, and mournful old Fish, who reported back once that three radio stations had beaten him to the arrest. He admired Mary Tyler Moore for letting the rest of the cast get most of the laughs. He knew Kiwis were annoyed by her shrill voice, but he felt they didn't appreciate her acting.

Americans, he says, were more mature with comedy. They worked harder at it, used more writers. Britain was in a bad patch. He sat in on the making of a *Doctor* episode and one of *Upstairs, Downstairs*, but he felt he learned much more in New York reading books on how to write plays. He had spent countless hours as he rewrote *Glide Time* four times.

It was written for the theatre because he felt that was where the risks were taken. Television was too careful. He was still smarting, he reluctantly confessed, about *In View of the Circumstances* being dropped after six shows. People told him it got better and better, yet it had been produced in a different sequence from the one shown. This proved to him it was just a question of people getting used to a show. After all, *Family at War* had almost flopped, but because 13 episodes had been bought, it was around long enough to catch on.

Perhaps, I suggested, people out at television should take a look at *Glide Time*, where you can hear a lot of people laughing?

Eventually, years later, they did. For many years *Gliding On*, the television series, was as popular in Kiwi homes as anything from Britain or America. The passing of the actor who played Jim from Stores was almost an occasion for national mourning. Roger got his West End success, and the movie of the play, and has gone on and on to make more Kiwis laugh than maybe any other person. Circa Theatre was able to pay for new seats from the profits from *Glide Time*. Roger achieved something nobody else before him and not many after him – he got Kiwi bums on our theatre seats.

When a local theatre is declining, they put on another Roger Hall play. This astute Pom has always been good with his titles, and it was little wonder that he called his memoirs *Bums on Seats*. He's the only person I know who specified a precise ambition and fulfilled it. He has made me, along with most New Zealanders, laugh more than any other local comedy writer. Except, I had the privilege of his wit for some student years morning, noon and night. I still think he should revive his wonderful comic impersonation of Kiwi Keith Holyoake. Roger has made a career out of puncturing our pretensions and pinning down our silly ways, and there was no Kiwi sillier or more pretentious than Kiwi Keith. Roger got him right, the affection for this idiot who represented us in the 1960s. It took a Pom then and now to put the laugh into our public persona.

The Caring, Controversial All Black Forward

Ken Gray was the first All Black, the first rugby player, to bring politics openly into sport. It was a brave move in the 1970s, marching as a member of HART (Halt All Racist Tours), lambasted by the aggressive Prime Minister Muldoon and called traitor by the Mayor of Dunedin. Not of course, to Ken's face. That would have been foolish. Ken was a very big man. He commanded respect, for his deeds on the rugby field and off it. He was a gentle giant of a farmer who never moved far from his roots and did as much as anybody to halt our racist tours.

Ken Gray offered a mercifully soft handshake. Thank God. His hands are built like bionic shovels. I confess I approached this interview gingerly. Mervyn Davies had just chosen him in his World XV, at a time when a Welshman might reasonably pack his choice team with Welsh forwards. But Gray was the most ferocious forward many of us had seen, even in the same team as Kel Tremain, Waka Nathan and Colin Meads.

The face is like a skull, on-field sporting the supremely confident snarl of a Celtic warrior, a man the nation was awesomely grateful was on our side in the 50 games he played for the All Blacks in the 1960s. We actually lost two of those games. I'm not sure how. Whineray and Lochore were our supreme generals, Meads and MacEwan jumping, Nathan and Tremain prowling like panthers, and Gray the best scrummager in the game, a bonus, no better jumper at the front of the lineout. Gray vied through the sixties with Meads as our most athletic and indomitable forward.

In the next decade he wrecked his amateur career. He

refused to play against the racially selected Springboks. This man who had caught his rugby fever from the famous 1956 Springbok tour of New Zealand, turned his broad back on the Everest of the game, the chance to go over there and beat them for the first time in their own backyard.

His new amateur occupation through the 1970s was as one of the most outspoken critics of South African rugby. It was 1977 when I drove out to meet this fourth-generation Plimmerton farmer who lives in a road bearing the family name, married to a fifth-generation lass from down the road. It is ridiculous to suggest traitorous intent from this man of the land.

Ken is soft-spoken about his hard-hitting opinions. Like his father before him, he is a local councillor, with aspirations to stand for Labour in the local electorate. He sees no discrepancy between politics and sport. He enjoys both. It was in fact the day of the Second Test, and Ken had been on television talking about the decline in scrummaging power.

He confessed to still feeling competitive, but he tried to damp it down. He agreed you had to be competitive to achieve a goal, but was that enough to make you a balanced person?

We went in to lunch. His wife, Joy, was in the kitchen in a kaftan, serving up curried pasta and cabbage. Their daughter Jane was at the table drawing. She liked riding ponies. Sons Andrew and John were off playing soccer.

Ah, soccer?

Ken smiled calmly. There is absolutely no stress in this man. No sign of that famous on-field scowl. He said his lads had played a little rugby, but they let them play what they wanted. Soccer was popular in the area, the immigrants were keen on it. He says there is more for kids now than in his day, when rugby was it.

More for the adults now too, not just beer or sweet sherry, like the reasonably dry local wine he uncorks, as he surveys the history of the game leading up to the'56 tour. He talks about our intense desire to beat the Boks, having been thrashed in '37, again in '49, when we thought we had the best team ever. So '56 was payback time.

There was also, said Joy, a closer feeling between South Africa and New Zealand than between other countries we played against. We were both nations of small, pioneering farmers, rugged people. You know, she adds, I didn't like the Lions much.

Pommie bas ... er, twits. Public-school types. Grass him, chaps, that sort of thing?

Well, says Ken mildly, it's a bit ambivalent. You find some of those hard-core Boers a bit hard to take. Yet we always have players wanting to go back there. You rarely hear of any wanting to go back to Britain.

Ken helped himself to another plate of pasta and cabbage.

You know, he continued, this argument about contact breaking down barriers, so we should go and play them. I think it is all to their benefit, that it creates an over-sympathy for them. And a tour is no way to see a country. You go from hotel to training field to booze-up. You only get to see the show parts. I guess it was much the same on my trip to China; you only see what they want you to see. But I don't want to bitch about the game. In '56 I really felt the desire to beat the Boks.

Really! Joy chides him fondly. You never told me that. But I do remember the excitement too. We were an hour late getting to Wellington Girl's because we had gone to see the Springboks arrive. We had never done anything like that before. It was just the big thing to do.

But, Ken sticks to his argument, it's not always true to say tours create goodwill. Look at Indian/Pakistan hockey matches. It's a form of nationalism.

The Olympics, Joy chimed in. You only watch your own country.

The attitude in Wales, says Ken sadly, sometimes made the All Black teams bitter. And yet, I suppose without the rugby, would the two countries have any contact? It is some form of bond. You know, I don't think it was Soweto and black problems that turned New Zealanders against South Africa this time, it was that dirty Third Test. Dirty South African bastards, people said. We should never have gone there.

There is a modified version of the comprehensive playing scowl, his massive brow descending like Venetian blinds. I would say, he says firmly, that the moderate New Zealander still tends to rationalise the events there, thinking the workers are looked after well and provided with a home. On tour I would say even the Maoris fraternise with the whites and do not associate emotionally with the blacks.

What about back home? His brow forms another layer of furrows. Well, basically there are the two camps, those against contact, those for contact, the latter much quieter about it. It's mysterious to me that National have reached the same position by stealth without using Labour's big stick to stop tours. You can see it in the leaders. Rowling is more typical of the average rugby enthusiast. He coached Going. And yet Muldoon, who is not a good mixer, has claimed the image of the typical Kiwi. I would say even Labour rugby supporters regard Muldoon as their man. Politics is like rugby, one team in red, one team in blue.

A broad smile threatens to crack the skull-face in half. It reminds me, he says, of that famous Athletic Club supporter. For 40 years he yelled for that club in Wellington, because Cliff Porter, All Black captain and Athletic player, had given him a ticket outside the park one day.

You would be on the red side?

Oh, Ken protests just a little, I am an independent on council. I got involved in local politics over an environmental issue, the proposal for a local emergency sewage outfall in the harbour. We managed to stop that.

He is both pleased at the successful start to his political career but relieved too that it happened. The local politics, he says, saved me from becoming a rugby heavy.

Rugby was so chauvinist, Joy objects. Still is. The sexes shouldn't be segregated. The youngsters won't put up with it.

Nor would Ken. I can't credit he would ever have ended up in the rugby club till all hours, reliving old scores over endless jugs of beer. Ken is a family man, a wine man, a thoughtful man, environmentally and politically aware, hopefully the way we are going.

I had suffered financially after 12 years in rugby, he admits. And you miss out in family ways. But rugby is better at club level now. It is the top administrators who are still so conservative. They could learn a lot from Petone Club, with its mixed social facilities and imaginative ideas, like the Champion of Champions.

Ken reckons the problem is that rugby is professional in every way except being professional. It demands huge dedication, time and employers' goodwill, which is no longer there. He reckons the game reached its amateur peak in the 1960s, when the All Blacks were fired up by the huge support, the thousands of telegrams.

We were not going to lose, he says, or we would get bad-mouthed in the pub later.

He doubts if doctors, for instance, like Hugh Barry and Tony Davies, would be able to be All Blacks now. And nor is there the same interest, with hundreds of schoolkids coming to watch an All Black training session. Now there are cars, boats, bikes, skiing.

He pauses to pop in a wedge of Camembert.

I take the opportunity to interrupt his analysis. Did his political retirement affect his relationship with other players? He nods. A close friend put a lot of distance between us.

On the other hand, Bob Scott, who was emotionally pro-South Africa, told me straight how disappointed he was in me. Yet we maintained our mutual respect.

He also denies he was first to protest. Des Webb, the North Auckland hooker, pulled out in 1960, Gerald Kember and Chris Laidlaw said they did not support future tours. But I suppose my announcement was seen by many as a betrayal. Rugby players felt undermined.

Still?

Well, since the Olympics, I think New Zealanders are seeing they can't remain in the backwoods. They realise they have to reassess their priorities. I never doubted the justification for my stand. We should see the political fact that the All Blacks are seen to represent us abroad.

We shouldn't, says Joy, offer any official support.

We're committed to that by Gleneagles, says Ken. It remains to be seen whether Muldoon draws back from that and raises the nationalistic paranoia.

He apologises for not being able to continue talking, as he has to drive to a studio interview. So we walk through the sitting-room. Among the modern New Zealand prints is an old oil of the original Gray homestead and a photograph of the clan. One of the black Scots. In the centre is his Scottish grandmother, who lived to 90. In the background is the veranda. Modernising, he says disgustedly, got rid of the old veranda.

We stand on the front lawn looking at the inner harbour and the soft green hills beyond. You know, he says, black eyes gleaming, this is the first year we've had black swans up here. We have all sorts of species – blue herons, pied oystercatchers, stilts. That brown swamp grass is rare. Up at our other farm at Pukerua we have a rare skink.

We walk past his muddy farm bike to his car. The farm dogs, Bing, Glen, Tan and Sue, follow at the respectful distance.

I suppose, he says, I'm a mixture – conservative and liberal. I wonder whether we can control either commerce or the unions. A guy develops a new vaccine but we are beholden to a multinational to market it. I've had my best year ever, good growth, good prices. The country's had a good year, yet the books don't balance.

A neighbour hailed Ken, wanting to borrow a chainsaw. Ken excused himself, saying he'd talked 90 percent rubbish.

When he was back, he launched into how disturbed he felt that South Africans regarded us as brothers under the skin. I would like, he says sombrely, to see us take a moral stand. We should have some basic principles we believe in. We should oppose contact for our own self-respect. I'd be interested in New Zealand doing more than just approve the Gleneagles agreement. Look at the way our aid programme has slipped from 0.7 in Kirk's time to under 0.5 now. I feel Kirk's cancellation of the tour was one of the few unpolitical gestures we have had in this country, done purely for principle.

Big Norm, Big Ken, two men of strong principle. We lost an opportunity to see Ken on the national stage when the grey successors to Kirk forced their man into the electorate where all the locals wanted Ken Gray. They knew he would serve them well. We can only guess how well he might have served his country again. We do know what a colossus he was as an All Black between 1963 and 1969. Chris Laidlaw said Meads was the last of a species. Gray was probably the link to the next generation, a great athlete and a progressive farmer who lived by his principles.

The Uncivil Kiwi Servant
of a Thousand Faces

Our stifling old public service provoked some notable eccentrics. Every weekday lunchtime for many years a grey suit would remove his jacket, fold it across his briefcase, stand on his hands and walk and up down Central Wellington's Plimmer Steps. Former Woburn Railway Workshop employee Govert van Herk became a Rawleigh Man selling unguents on 30-centimetre high, spring-loaded stilts, warming to the job with early morning flights along Eastbourne's main street powered by a dynamo attached to his left leg with lightweight plastic wings adding speed and control. But most pervasive of all was the top salesman for Government Life Insurance, predecessor of Tower Insurance. Ron Megget's calling card launched the country's 60,000 public servants into the annual Meggetattack, defacing and displaying on noticeboards around the land the endless permutations possible with a pen applied to poor Ron's grey dial. Even today with only 20,000 public servants, the many bizarre Meggetfaces are fondly remembered as small bright stars in those grey public service skies.

Ron Megget by 1975 had had enough. He declared war on parliamentarians. The cake-cutters, he calls them. At the age of 61, the supremely grey and properly invisible senior insurance agent for Government Life was standing up to be counted, as Feminist candidate for the electorate of Island Bay. He vowed to use every legal guerilla tactic he could think of. Here are some of them.

The first salvo was delivered, so to speak, outside Parliament. Standing comfortably and almost unnoticed among the young and mostly female pro-abortion lobbyists was this mild-looking, middle-aged male in the greyest of suits cut as conservatively as any Customs Department clerk's. The significant difference was that Ron was waving gigantic knitting needles above his head, symbolising the potential for parliamentarians to vote a return to the backstreet or self-induced abortion.

He waited patiently for his turn to speak. Ignorant men telling lies, he said, jabbing the needles at the soft underbelly of an institution most of whose members did not look much different from himself, except their suits were better cut.

Back among the heavy mild steel filing cabinets of his Government Life office he was not backtracking, proving the point by removing from among the hundreds of insurance forms in his bulging briefcase the knitting needles with which he punctuates his political points. He looks calm enough, but he has not calmed down.

Parliament on abortion, he says, jabbing the needles sharply in the direction of the nation's lawmakers. Men telling women what to do with their bodies. That's what politicised me. Specifically my MP for Island Bay, Gerald O'Brien. Here it is ...

He relinquishes his knitting needles long enough to extract Hansard from a drawer, flip to the marked section.

Blah. Blah. Right, page 861. O'Brien: A widely-held fallacy that a Member of Parliament must represent the views of his constituents.

Ron looks up. If I understand English, he says heavily, the House of Representatives consists of people who represent their constituents.

He accepts he will not get in at Island Bay. Not the point, he says, reaching for his knitting needles. The premium is on making one helluva din. His second salvo, here it is: his pro-abortion pamphlet, appearing under his mother's name Rona Calverley, to shield the Family Planning Association, you understand. Ron has been president of that association for the last 17 years, running the biggest birth control clinic in the country, with 6500 patients.

It's not abortion on demand, he insists. It's abortion in desperation, for 10,000 New Zealand women every year.

My first premise, he explains, is based on the old Roman dictum: You no playa da game, you no maka da rules.

And that's actually in the pamphlet?

Ron proudly nods yes. His kind of boisterous, jokey pamphleteering surely belongs in an Evelyn Waugh satire. But he is saying it in Parliament's face, calling them bloody LIARS!!

Ron, isn't this maybe libellous, outside the House?

Ron is not fazed. Blame A.H. Reed, he suggests. He was my Sunday-School teacher. I believe in gimmicks. I have a score of them in my briefcase.

Parliament is becoming familiar with Ron's gimmicks. Last year the Superannuation Commission was confronted with an unusual submission, a kumara boiled in an electric jug in front of the committee and handed to the chairman with the words: 'I now hand you this hot potato.'

Remember Richard John Seddon, Ron imperturbably explains. Remember where he came from! Kumara! On the West Coast. He was one of the last liberal politicians we had. He set up a decent old-age pension. I invited those jokers in Parliament to pick up the mantle of Seddon.

Up until now Ron has not gone public, in deference to his wife's pleas. Well, not that public. He has been dabbling in local politics, school and hospital, National Party ground-roots stuff.

However, Ron has always been very public in his profession. He has made a face for himself known the length and breadth of every public service office in the land. Go into any government department, find the noticeboard and you find Ron in his many guises, bringing out the schoolboy defacer you might not have thought existed behind the reluctant exterior of the nation's bureaucrats. On every noticeboard you see the anonymous and merciless caricatures imposed on Ron Megget's insurance man's calling card.

I keep the best ones at home, says Ron with unblinking pride. Hitler. Nasser. Muldoon.

Wasn't there some kind of competition?

Absolutely. Every year I judged the best Megget. Up at Industries and Commerce.

And were there any other developments with the Megget?

Most assuredly. At the time of all the protest about the Bomb, there was the Meggetron. There was a Meggetwatt in the New Zealand Electricity Department. There was Meggetomania. All good for business.

The business of defacing Megget is probably as pervasive and compulsive among bureaucrats as the reading of the Bristow cartoon strip about the pathetic little office worker whose only friends seem to be pigeons. Most of the efforts, of course, are like Bristow, pathetic. Around Broadcasting on my rounds for the *Listener* I passed the Megget parade, the Van Dyck beards, the Groucho glasses, the Genghis Khan helmet, the Captain Cook hat, the Laughing Cavalier full headdress, the John Lennon rimless glasses look, the Pope or maybe Rabbi skullcap millinery and the depilated, tonsured and/or lobotomised monk, inevitably a good few nuns, always with Ron's only prominent feature, his up-raised eyebrows, heavily inked along the Groucho lines. Really, Ron looks as unremarkable as any of his defacers, just another grey suit, bland face, tidy hair, public servant, as tepid as Alec Guinness off stage. Put him up on his little office screen and Ron is transformed as astonishingly and as differently as any Guinness canon of eccentric characters.

Ron is really just the putty in his potential clients' hands. He does the rounds of every public office in the land, distributing his card, noting how eagerly the cards are snapped up. He has no idea how many he has distributed over a traditional four-decade life sentence as a public servant. A lot. A good little earner for some jobbing printer.

So where does his wily promotional style come from? Did he perchance set the ball rolling, dispensing his own caricatures of himself? Ron has nothing to say on that, except that it just seemed to gain its own momentum.

So where then lies the secret of his success as the nation's best-known insurance salesman, the visible many, many faces of what seems in our entrenched public service to be scarcely a pressing requirement, insurance for those assured a job from school to retirement?

Ron leans on his bulging briefcase, letting the silence do the work. Yes, in his briefcase, those gimmicks. Maybe there are secrets there? Or is it his bland face, the *tabula rasa* on which I confess I have written my own script as much as any other public servant. I too have defaced Ron. But that is not what this interview is about.

So what about your parents? I ask desperately.

My father was a Dunedin businessman, he says. My mother worked as a secretary for Truby King, typing on train trips to and from the dairy herd his theories on milk, which led to the Plunket Society.

Ah, clues at last. Yes, he conceded, he got from his mother his lifelong absorption in social work.

And from his father his business head.

But where did the gimmicks come from?

I am an aberration as a New Zealander, says Ron. I am of Hugenot stock. There's gold in us. Ancestor Louis Michelle struck it in Victoria. I inherited money, I married into money, I made money. I could comfortably retire to the Pukerua Bay bach, where I swim six months of the year.

He pauses. Maybe I'm mad, he concedes, but somebody has to spur women on to stand up for their rights. If a guy with my money and my little ability goes out and plays golf, democracy in this country will sink.

All is not lost. So far 40 people have offered to help him conduct an urban guerilla gimmick war against the cake-cutters. He knows the female half of the electorate will be watching him pull the chair out from under the sitting member. More Meggetpower is promised from this serious joker.

Update: Ron retired to his Pukerua Bay bach.

A Galumphing Kiwi Poet
Called Glover

James K. Baxter holds the high ground as our premier serious, if not seriously tormented, poet. Mason and Fairburn slot in as our Angry Young Depression poets. There are roadie performing pub poets with a current following. None inspire everyday quotes like 'quardle oodle ardle wardle doodle', Denis Glover's magpie-speak. Every few weeks you will hear it or a 'Sings Harry' companion piece set to Douglas Lilburn's music on the Concert Programme. That canny old silver jubilee's worth of a poet from his Depression possie third behind Mason and Fairburn right up until his death in the early 1980s, writing deceptively light and simple poems and ditties about Wellington harbour out his front window, is proving to be lasting the literary distance better than most. I caught him as usual at it in 1975.

Denis Glover is sitting mid-morning at his desk by the window, looking over Wellington harbour. He was sitting there at dawn, watching the sun rise over Eastbourne, sipping on a flagon of something potent, rereading Boswell on Johnson, feeding the birds, writing his poems to the harbour.

The sun, says the poet, drifts across to the Hutt as the seasons flow and the world rolls.

He pauses for another drink.

Which way, dear boy, does the sun rise? Eh?

He is addressing my colleague, illustrator Bob Kerr. Reluctantly, Bob looks up from an illustrator's dream, that lined and pitted facequake.

What's yer name, eh? persists the playful poet. Kerr?

Cur? Car? Care? I prefer Cur. Only that cook fellow was Care. People sometimes call me Clover.

What about Plover, a gregarious bird?

Speaking on behalf of Sir Isaac Newton, he says in measured tones, eyes sharp as any magpie's, though the rest of his face could be mistaken for a piece that has fallen off Mount Cook all the way down to the Canterbury Plains where he once excelled as a boxer, perhaps explaining a condition akin to many blows with a blunt rake. Speaking for Sir Isaac, it is not true that the sun rises in the east and sets in the west. The world rolls west to east, and it wobbles to make the seasons.

I'm not responsible, he adds with an indifferent sniff, reaching for his snuffbox. He doesn't explain, just observes the world, from an acute angle to starboard, or port. Port! Where's the vodka? he bellows back to his wife, Lyn, who is busy pouring him another amberful glass from the flagon, something that is less ferocious than vodka, something out of one of those gargantuan barrels that line John Bull's downtown winery.

Denis is peering malevolently at the little yellow teddy bear on the sill. Reminds me of Churchill, he rumbles. Call 'im Winnie the Pooh.

He is fingering the paperweight with obviously evil intent. It is, in fact, a large piece of shrapnel which he understands was intended for him, so he keeps it handy. He served in the Navy during the war, including a sub-zero stint with the Russkies patrolling out of Murmansk, for which they gave him a medal. A fair bet he felt more common cause with vodka-swilling Russian sailors than with a Pommie strong on cigars and brandy.

The exploded iron paperweight does a reasonable job of containing piles of paper poems he confesses he never finishes sorting. Liquorice allsorts is his name for them. Curiously strong peppermints might be another name for them, given how many inspired the etchings that cover the back wall, quintessentially peculiar and fetching Glover lines like 'My love is an electrolux'.

What's the story with the kea? Carved out of kauri, sent to me by an old ex-naval commander after he heard me on Jim Henderson's radio programme *Open Country*.

Birds. Glover is never far from the subject. He got the magpie transliterated into 'quardle oodle ardle wardle doodle' in his 1940s poems, as it sat up in a tree watching Tom and Elizabeth lose their farm to the mortgage corporation.

I get, Glover proposed, a ... what's the word? ... yes, a plethora of birds on my veranda. Hence the bird fodder. He is fixing me with the beady magpie eye, glinting from the far end of a nose like a mutated turnip. He drains his glass, puts it down carefully, reverently, beside his poems, places his hands across his stomach like a barrister about to sum up the sorry story his client has just delivered.

Seagulls. Starlings. Sparrows. Waxies. He enumerates each species clearly. I feed them every morning. The sparrows chirp. The waxies look terrified, and hungry. The starlings say nothing. Just swoop and then beat it with the food. The seagulls never scream here. As a sailor I heard so many, they used to drive me mad. The morepork is the only bird I like in the New Zealand bush. By God, when I sit in the bush and hear that bird in the silence, there's nothing else ...

Glover cups his thumbs and blows the lonely owl-cry.

Very eerie, he says. That bird haunts my life.

It began early, he says. As a kid with an air-rifle, seeing this morepork. I was a deadly shot. I pumped three beebee pellets into it, one, two, three, reload, one , two, three. It took no notice. Finally ... with a great SHUFFE! ... it swooped down at my head. The morepork in the dark bush took so much from Glover, and then no more.

143

We have been taking Glover for half a century as poet, printer of poets and Boswell to his own Johnson with his breezy autobiography *Hot Water Sailor*. Glover described Johnson as a galumphing old maniac full of sententious rubbish and brilliant commonsense. Isn't that true of all of us? he asks.

Well, maybe of him. More contentious than sententious, a contrary poet with a magpie eye and an owl's ear.

Lest he give the wrong impression, he adds, he admires the good Doctor, not least for his acceptance of 10 guineas from a would-be subscriber to his dictionary, then informing him that there was no list of subscribers because he had spent the money. That is fair, Glover adjudges. We got the dictionary, Johnson got the money. Fair bargain Glover would settle for – we get his books, he gets our money.

Glover's brow furrows, extravagantly. A cloud has passed across his harbour. Prefer to read the traditional English poets, he growls. Current lot unaware of tradition. They don't know a bloody thing. Touring with some of them recently. Wouldn't bother twice with their stuff – fool rhymes and febrile choppings from the telephone book, all names and no plot, all mime and show, no half-rhymes and subtle assonance. But the $70 a week, liked that.

Another ripple deep and uneven as a discarded sheet of buckled, rusted-out corrugated iron moves across his brow. When we were young, he snaps, you borrowed a bike. Now they lay on a minibus. That breaks down, they ring for a helicopter.

A bit fanciful for the good Doctor, but certainly elements of Johnsonian scorn.

I haven't been nice, Glover says nastily, since I was a tweed-twitcher in the boy scouts.

He blamed the education system, the sausage factory, though he came out undigested, having traipsed the country from birth in Dunedin to Auckland Boys' Grammar to

Christ's College and Canterbury University, where boxing was the perfect outlet for his feelings about educational sausage factories. He did manage a BA, which is better than Baxter, who dipped out at Wellington's Victoria University and became a postie, though when I was there the rumour was they were studying Baxter poems in Stage Two English while Baxter was failing Stage One.

Glover was a tramper and a yachtie, after the war a journalist, typographer and publisher with Caxton Press in Christchurch, which he helped found. And used it to introduce New Zealanders to the joys of Baskerville type as well as what was set from him in the way of humorous and serious verse, sometimes both in the same typographical package. I recall his visit to Holy Name Seminary at the invitation of Father Bernard O'Brien SJ, who told us indifferent School Certificate English students that here was a true New Zealand poet. Glover imperturbably delivered 'Sings Harry' and earned from us the accolade we had scoffed at, not believing until then New Zealand had real poets.

Glover was real, all right. Like kina, rough on the outside, a salty celebration within, something you might get from a sushi bar, rank with iodine, packed with verbal protein. An oysterer roisterer, pickled in port, not always easy to digest.

I stayed undigested, he says with unrestrained glee. An odd fish, a no-hoper, among men a snapper, among women a groper – as I wrote once.

The only thing I want to do now, he snarled, is practise anti-aircraft fire at the low-flying planes dripping kerosene pollution all over the harbour. Although, he says ominously, reaching for the paperweight …

I am grateful I am not a low-flying plane. You have to take seriously a threat from a lad with a declared deadly aim, from a sailor who survived those Murmansk convoys.

Safely out the door, I could risk being the poetaster:

A galumphing Kiwi poet called Glover
Was not averse to being in clover.
His preference was birds
He could capture in words,
A debt we owe this artful plover.

Shona Kiwi Shooting Star

Shona Laing at an Auckland garden party in 1989, returned from her OE tilt at international recognition, was austere, remote and yet also commanding. She looked tougher. Others spoke on her unsolicited behalf, particularly about how she had sung with the huge rock band Manfred Mann and they gave her a raw deal. Since then she has been a regular performer around the country, seemingly content with her solid, somewhat stroppy folk/punk singer status. The caustic 'I'm Glad I'm not a Kennedy' won her new fans who probably would not bother with the flip side of her American commentary, her first and most memorable hit '1905', in praise of Henry Fonda, way back when her time was all ahead of her. She still has the quality she revealed then, a sensitive talent and a poise, like Joni Mitchell, or the other gal from the same bay, Katherine Mansfield. I interviewed her in 1975, when it was all ahead of her, maybe.

Shona Laing, one of our few good singer/songwriters, was talking about why she was leaving New Zealand. More correctly, her manager, Rick, was explaining on her behalf. She was looking a long way off, seeing something she might maybe sing about. Rick explained the move was all about the struggle to stay herself, to develop herself, and to him this had a lot to do with the availability of money. Like bread, man.

The rap was taking place in the white and yellow offices of a new record company Rick had svengalied together. Stripped wood desks. LPs lying about on the bare wood floor. Rick was laid back, almost outasight in a steep, three-sided canvas chair that looked like an oversized toddler's truss. Clumps of greying hair and calculator eyes under a black corduroy cap, zipped black boots swinging.

And Shona, she was crouched in a corner of the sofa in regulation denims, fiddling with her fingers, smoking too much, long hair round a friendly freckled face free of make-up. Plain, sturdy, natural and 19, by no stretch the 'petite Shona Laing' an ad proclaimed. Behind her was the framed gold disc for '1905'. She saw my glance. Just gold-plated, she said, smiling.

It was a gold-plated song, about Henry Fonda and time, time, time, introducing us to Shona's winsome, heartfelt songs of innocence and exhortation, to stop the hating and show your love, give up your masquerade in a good follow-up song and you'll be made.

'Have you ever seen,' she sang, 'how a touch makes people pull away? And to smile at a stranger's not the thing to do today.'

Longing in her voice: 'Is anything everlasting? ... even evergreen trees must lose their leaves one day.'

Flower power, tree power, green power, something the powerful dismiss as harmless hippie stuff.

Rick was talking, about taking Shona to Australia to record the next album so they could achieve like a 'total creative environment'. She murmured she sorta liked the first album, 'cos there was more relating. The second was like a job. But then, she said to Rick, maybe the first was too relaxed?

Yeah, the first hit, that was her making and unmaking. Too much success too soon. The sort of complaint the rest of us who will never have a hit do not relate to, though maybe the fact '1905' was played into the ground on radio was a bit much. Probably got more local airplay than 'Mull of Kintyre' would, and how often have you heard Paul McCartney singing that in the last few decades, huh?

She wasn't ready, Shona said. But, she couldn't stop the success. She was a conciliatory person. She tried to satisfy the demands of the system that stamps the individual into the polystyrene production line, suited to the wearing of white on endless cheery telly programmes. She tried charm school and she didn't; she got a letter saying she looked like a cow on the telly.

Ah, Shona, Rick says, you did get some tips at that charm school.

She just wanted to be allowed to be herself, Shona said, showing a stubborn jut to her jaw, not just wanting to please. But yeah, she nodded in the metronomic way of today's youth, she did go to that charm school of her own free will.

Rick saw the problem coming from the public not supporting its talent and the promoters not pushing. The public wouldn't pay more than two dollars for locals, but paid five or six for overseas artists. Promoters thought they were doing you a favour to book you, kept on about the publicity value. Shona got $30 a night touring with Kamahl; he probably got $3000.

Yeah, she said. The rip-off of all time.

Her first album sold 5000, he said, and her second over 2000. In England you could pull $1000 a week on the support of your record-buying public without being a star, but here you were at the top and then nothing. Where could John Hanlon go now after the huge hit 'Damn the Dam'? To be economically viable you had to do overseas imitations, like Space Waltz. Steve Allen was mainly restricted to cover versions. The media didn't help, using photos of overseas artists when they could have one of Shona, putting on an hour of Leon Russell when it could have been John Hanlon, using Kenny Rogers when they could have used a local for *Come Alive*.

Rick was getting angrier, rising off the canvas. Kenny Rogers hasn't done much for two years overseas, yet he cleans up maybe $100,000 in three months here. Why, he shouted, doesn't the government look at all the money overseas artists

149

are taking out?

Yeah, said Shona, nodding almost vigorously. There are better local groups than Paper Lace, but they don't get the promotion.

Shona's second album, *Shooting Stars Are Only Seen at Night*, was somewhat anti-commercial with ironic lines about 'straight-eyed men' who complain about their wives, 'bourbon talking' exhortation replaced by accusation, the flower power somewhat wilted. That was her growing pains, but not a pleasure to her public. She didn't have crushes, she said, on Henry Fonda any more. So it was off to London, where they felt she had room for both her feelings and her fortune. Grooming wouldn't matter there.

You'll have to make it on talent, kid, Rick told her. Unless, he added, we get you a facelift in Italy on the way.

Katherine Mansfield was also from the Bay and 19 and disgruntled with New Zealand when she left it for London. Shona physically was made of sterner stuff. She too had the talent to make it in the metropolis, which would be New Zealand's loss and everybody's gain.

The Playmaker of Kiwi Street Games

*Half a century ago a young New Zealand teacher wanted his pupils to relate to their own community, as opposed to the heavy emphasis on Mother Britain as the repository of all culture. Brian Sutton-Smith wrote about his own boyhood games in Wellington's seaside suburb of Island Bay in the book **Our Street**. It was the country's first realistic picture of Kiwi boys at play. Instead of having **Just William** or the **Famous Five** to read about, Kiwi kids had their own backyard. There was quite a controversy from the stern educators, but Kiwi kids loved it and still do. It is now a New Zealand classic. The next 25 or so books by this author were educational texts published in America, where he had to go, to Columbia University, to be able to become a professor of play. He still comes back regularly, and he still likes to stir the educational pot. I took him back to **Our Street**. Here the child demonstrably proved to be father of the man.*

Brin, as he called himself in the book, sat on the grassy slope outside Number 12. Nothing much had changed, except for the trams. This was how he put it at the end of *Our Street*:

'Everything would be quiet and peaceful. Here and there a dog would bark or a tram go by, and nobody would say anything for a long, long time. The grasshoppers would sing in the grass, and the sun would stream down, and Brin and Smitty and Gormie and Horsey would just close their eyes and let the sun seep through their skin.'

It was that kind of day. Really hot. Crickets and grasshoppers competing. We sat there chewing on straws of dried grass, soaking it in. This was it. I had read *Our Street* as a lad in the Bay of Plenty, loved it as the first book that really spoke to me about us. I went on to become a teacher and read the book to pupils. I wrote my version about me and Mike and Gary growing up in a small Bay of Plenty village, *The Kid from Matata*. Now I was actually here, in Our Street, with its author.

His recall was perfect, as he lay on the grass, his slightly dishevelled hair the colour of the dried grass around us, his face open with boyish pleasure.

The big fence has gone as well as the trams, he said. Still all those Island Bay dogs barking everywhere, the same tangle of power lines carving up the skyline, the old wooden houses with white paling fences. Down the end of the street there, he nodded, the garage remains, where we played cricket and got told off if we got on the roof.

His wife, Shirley, was six years behind him at Island Bay school, and he ended up teaching her as a student teacher. He got to know her when she became a student teacher back here, when he was researching children's games for serious tomes like *The Games of New Zealand Children* and *Play with Your Children*. He has had dozens of scholarly honours for his work, been inducted into half a dozen societies of his peers, presides as programme head for departmental psychology at Teachers College, Columbia University, New York, while his five children have grown up there. And now he is being invited back here to lecture, having proved himself abroad. He doesn't get brickbats anymore from our educators.

They flew thick and fast about his head when he was only known as the author of *Our Street* and its sequel *Smitty Does a Bunk*. There was just no precedent for our educators being able to cope with such unbridled challenges to adult authority as street scraps, breaking a cat's saucer with a cricket ball, sneaking into flicks for free, references to 'sissies' and 'rotten cows'. To our Victorian educators these were subversive and wilfully juvenile.

How times change. Now there is a year-long waiting list for his books with the National Children's Library Service. So many teachers have told his publishers, Price Milburn, that no other books go down better in the classroom. The good news for classrooms is that Brin wrote a third in the series, *Smitty and Brin*, taking the larrikins from Island Bay on to Form Three at Wellington College.

I started the first book, he says, when I was teaching eight-year-olds, and I was struck with the lack of anything in their reading matter that was like the world around them or the way they thought.

My father was a postmaster and told us stories as kids. I had to interrupt to tell Brin my father was also a postmaster who told us stories when we were kids.

Brin topped that. My father's father, he said, was a saddlesmith. He gathered the family round the stove on Sunday evenings to make up stories.

I said meekly I remembered my Irish Nana by the coal-range pulling us up on her lap and giving us big hugs and telling us stories and singing us songs. But I wasn't sure what Granddad did, he sort of hovered about in the background.

Brin continued. Without thinking about it consciously, when I came into the same situation as a teacher, I started doing the same thing. I was recollecting 1934 for kids in 1946. Their enthusiasm was so damn strong for us kids sitting on porches and picking away with pistols, more or less in their lingo, probably causing much the same minor disruptions in the community, they wanted a chapter each day. I had to go like heck to provide a new one each day, and that's what dragged the book out of me.

I'll bet. I told Brin about the potato guns that fired a potato pellet captured when mum wasn't looking, the rubberband guns, big pink rubberbands from the works, the Maori kids carving revolvers out of wood just like Audie

Murphy used in *Billy the Kid*, the shanghai fights. Whoops, I was breaking the cardinal rule – interviewers should ask questions and not be heard. Brin didn't mind. I guess he was used to kids and folk burbling on to him about their games.

The nice thing about him is that despite all those heavy-duty books, he is full of the same unaffected, boyish enthusiasm that his Smitty and Brin stories communicate. He is relaxed, his snappy red American collegiate blazer folded up to use as a headrest.

My older brother and I, he says happily, were the real street-Arab phase. Both my parents came from farming and small-town areas, coming into city life. They were decent and honourable, but they really didn't have much idea about kids. In their day kids were completely gripped into a farm culture, doing all sorts of necessary chores. When people like that come into a city, they don't think of doing anything with their children, so their kids roam pretty wild.

He pauses to confess he is rehearsing his lecture. The next phase of historical growth, he says, chewing on a dry stalk, is that the kids of these kids have parents who organise them more, into football, dancing, music. I think there was more freedom in our childhood because we were a generation hanging between rural upbringing and more adequate, more considered city life.

Brin is really in lecture mode now. The stalk is used as a pointer. The greatest variety of games in New Zealand, he declares, was from 1890, when there were enough people and enough complexity of life, up to about 1920. Variety began to decrease with the growing homogeneity of communities. With increasing wealth more kids of upper-class status are going to lessons. A domestication of the community is going on, and with it a loss of games, like tops, marbles, knives, hopscotch, Saddle the Nag.

These relics of older cultures filled the gap until new

resources were created by society, civilised alternatives such as reading, movies, television. With television there has been a terrific escalation of symbolic activities. Kids today quite often don't play vigorously at all. They're fantastic at games of strategy, what the chess world championship conflict is all about, chess as sport, a very exciting one, largely through the television coverage.

And don't, I spontaneously insert, forget *Pot Black*.

He has seen most change in the classroom. School is no longer the 'gates of misery' it was for Smitty and Brin, where teacher is the enemy, to the underside of whose desk you nail rotten fish.

He has risen off the hallowed Brin turf to deliver the core of his argument. Our attachment to the work ethic, he says, continues to prevent us accepting the importance of play. I have switched my concern to pre-school play. We shield children from the fantasy of devastation, which is what they feel. Children feel powerless, they fantasise so they can feel powerful. They need to go through four phases of fantasy growth, from terror to escape to combat to victory. They do so by telling stories, in ascending order of difficulty. It is what Levi Strauss says about myths for us all: we spin a tale about what we fear. It does not get rid of the threat, but it does distance it. Then we tell another because the threat is still there. Adults structure what they think children should hear. If children are restricted by adult concepts of what they should like, they do not develop imaginatively, therefore their personality is hampered.

I take this dire warning lying down. I will not any longer object to my daughter's insatiable diet of Babysitters' Club stories, maybe several hundred paperbacks at last count. I know it was okay to read her Grimms Fairy Stories like Dad read to Mike and me, that got her and us through the terror of the giants and ogres, which she escaped with my help. I did get sick of reading her the manger story by Jan

155

Pienkowski, even though this dark rendering of Christmas was exquisitely drawn. I think the stories I told her about Horace-Thomas the magic horse rescuing animals from zoo captivity was combat and victory. So now she was on her own kick, with girl power, though she said it was nice of me to put Horace-Thomas into a book for her.

Brin or the prof, or both, brought me back to earth, or grass, talking about his awe and respect for the mystery of child's play, this dark continent we still barely perceive. The game that puzzled me most, he said, pointing. I sat up, eager to hear a secret revealed, still I guess a kid at heart. It was the one, he said, we played there in the street. It started me doing my PhD thesis.

What? What was it?

A crazy little kid's game called 'Who Tipped the Finger?' You play it in Standard One or Two. One kid stands with his finger behind his back and the others stand behind him. One says: 'North, south, east, west, draw a snake down your back and who tipped your finger?'

Brin remembers when he went teaching seeing the game in operation in the playground. He wondered what the hell was going on. Then the recognition of having played the game got him going on his lifelong professional quest to discover what children's games are all about. I still, he concedes, don't know who tipped the finger.

He has peeled back one secret layer, only to reveal deeper layers, the dark areas where the child is father of the man. This is where most of his present interest is absorbed.

Brin and Smitty are actually a relief for him, from this difficult quest. Allowing kids to fight, he says, goes all the way back to needing dispensable manpower, when what they did mainly with young men was kill them, sacrifice them, make them heroes. If they were good at this, they were terrible to live with, drunken, active, delinquent – but terrific to die for. I had a flash of our league players, dispensable after a few brutish seasons of this collision sport.

Today, Brin says, kids show more initiative in the verbal and symbolic areas, less in the physical. We're training a nation of computer managers, not a nation of fighters, as middle and upper-class American boys in Vietnam demonstrated. Kids are still thinking war, but in terms of space ships and button pushing, the distancing from the victim that was such a horrible part of the Vietnam war.

Television is an interference, he says, getting my full attention, given my concern at the endless videos my daughter and friends watch. But he is still in preschool. *Sesame Street,* he says, had to get across to kids the basically stupid task of understanding numbers, so it could get the Ford millions to make the programmes. It has, of course, transformed this idiocy. The most valuable part of the programme is those playful puppets.

Big Bird, Miss Piggy, take a bow!

If, he says, frowning, we could just let those imaginative *Sesame Street* people do what they do so imaginatively – instead of communicating GARBAGE!

Right, I said, sitting up straight.

If, he persisted, you develop the imagination up to age 11, imaginative 11-year-olds pick up the Three Rs overnight, as just another game.

He shakes his head. His mother used to object he only put into his books the things his parents didn't want him to do, which was hardly representative of the good boy he was most of the time.

He analyses that. The whole tendency of civilisation, he explains, is to secure against war and panic and plague. But with the security you get dullness. The meaning for me of modern life is searching for ways to make life vivid. Play is a vivification of experience.

Personally, I would settle for being good at cricket.

If we weren't working, he says, I'm sure we would spend

157

just as much time as children in play, seeking vivid experiences. The maids of Queen Elizabeth I played tag and other chasing games that kids still play, and were just as serious about them.

The children of Queen Elizabeth II play tag games too, but they seem to end usually in tears.

The children in my classroom, he says, encouraged me to rediscover my vivid experiences. Now I am passing on the message I learned from my pupils.

Well, he has succeeded in spades pour *moi*. It feels really vivid sitting on this grassy bank, sun streaming down, eyes closed, everything peaceful except for a dog barking.

Yeh, Brin, I murmur, there was this time the whole school had this humungous shangai fight down the sandhill and ...

The Brightest Eye
on Our Dark Land

Brian Brake is our most famous photographer. Most of his professional life he was in great international demand, his series for Life magazine on the Indian monsoon one of the most famous of all photo essays. His book New Zealand: Gift of the Sea remains the benchmark of local landscape photography and has never been out of print in four decades. As a journalist, I worked with Brake on an assignment for a London magazine on Wanganui Collegiate where Prince Edward was to tutor. We spent all day at the college, and he took many photos. After dinner we were retiring to our hotel when Brake, who never went anywhere without his camera, said he was just ducking back to the college. But it'll be lights out for the boarders? I haven't got that, he said. I have to get it all. This from a man whom I thought had come back to New Zealand to retire. Wrong. He had his piece of land in Titirangi, but retirement was never an option. There was too much to photograph, to celebrate. He had to photograph it all.

You could take Brian Brake for a motelier. He has an open, agreeable face, thinning sandy hair swept back revealing many freckles, an amiable smile, attentive without being pushy. He is unobtrusive. And when you work with him, you realise he is emotionally committed to getting inside his subjects.

I was never any good at advertising photography, he confesses. In London I once tried to do a wrapped bottle of gin. It was a disaster. To me the subject matter has to say something. Even when I am photographing still life, say a pot, the pot has to dominate. You become attached to your subject, even to Egyptian mummies. When I was photographing the gold mask of Tutankhamen in Paris, the old cleaning lady came in on the last day of the exhibition and said goodbye to the mask.

For me, the inside cover shot in *New Zealand: Gift of the Sea,* looking up through the green semi-transparent umbrella of a spread ponga, was a shock of recognition: yes, this is our land. Brake connected us to our land. Some of the strongest images in this strong, durable and somewhat shadowy book of our dark land, if one can single any out, are of kauri, ponga, driftwood, sheep on hill country.

Yes, he says, I have a couple of kauri at my Titirangi place. But my own favourites were the farmers at the Kumeu A & P Show and the two boys and a girl on a cliff at Tauranga. I say was, because they have dropped them from the revised edition. Probably a commercial reason that the boys have short-back-and-sides haircuts. I'm not bitter about them being removed. The whole book could be dropped. I'm surprised it has gone on so long.

Brian is modest and matter-of-fact in the understated Kiwi way, but it does not disguise his absorption in his craft. I like the stark quality of the open New Zealand spaces, he says, but I like the people more. I'd like to do the book again, get the look of New Zealanders the way they've changed and yet not changed. Of course, there would be no reproduction of situations. I never do that. It's fatal for me, anything posed.

It was the wide-open, stark, rugged spaces of the McKenzie Country that got him a job with the famous freelance group of photographers called Magnum. Typically perhaps for a resourceful Kiwi, he was not fazed about approaching the most famous photographers in the world and asking for a job. He got it and also a quick, critical lesson from Magnum photographer Ernest Haas, who praised his colour photography but wryly enquired, 'By the way, do any people live in New Zealand?' Ever since, Brake has been a people photographer, seeking the critical moment the most famous Magnum photographer, Henri Cartier-Bresson, espoused.

There were only a select 17 Magnum photographers, and the world was their oyster. Young Brian was soon among more people than the McKenzie Country has sheep, drawn to the crowds of Asia. What jolted me out of the salon approach to photography, he says, was the visual shock of seeing so many people having to live so close together in Singapore. My eyes started to roam, to see people, and then I had to record it. You have to live with your subject.

His Asian pictures, most notably his study of the monsoon in India, made his name. *Life* magazine was sceptical about sponsoring the project, he recalls, but they agreed to first rights. When they saw the pictures, they splashed them over 20 pages, just ahead of *Paris Match* and *Queen*.

The key to his success lay in his intense and prolonged research, a year through 1958-9, talking to many people including the famous Indian film director Satyajit Ray.

You are a thief, he says of the job. You are prying, though people usually know I am around. Like the Indian woman with the rain streaming down her face. She was one of Ray's actresses and she knew I was on the set, roaming around, but not exactly where. This became one of the most famous photographs in the world. Nehru asked to see the pictures, said he didn't know how Brake had come to know India so well.

Brake put in the time, the hard yakka, lived with Indian families. I partook of their life, he says, because if you photograph in a country, you have to understand it. His still pictures of his monsoon sequence were full of movement, life and colour, because he had studied carefully the records of the monsoon and knew what he was trying to achieve. Study, concentration, application, immersion, persistence and the unobtrusive, easy-going, sticky-beak Kiwi approach that gets in close without getting people's backs up.

I think there is something in our New Zealand character that breaks barriers, he observes, even if it is by accident. For example, not knowing you should have your shoes off and, as a result, capturing the moment. You must always be ready for the moment. It is tiring, but you have to do it.

The Cartier-Bresson philosophy – but married to a determined, resolute Kiwi approach, prepared to rough it and take as long as it takes to get the job done. Brian was well prepared for this. He grew up looking at the mountains from Arthur's Pass, where his father ran the general store. He was befriended by an old Scotsman, Charlie Warden the ranger. Brian remembers Charlie making his own slides and showing them on a lantern slide projector, using a Fijian spear as a pointer to the different kinds of native bush. He had all these marvellous old cameras, wooden, no bellows, using wet plates and Cooks lens. I was accused of lifting a box Brownie when I was 10 or 11. I used it to photograph the landscape.

Brake's next major influence could not have been more different, the portrait and studio-bound photographer Spencer Digby.

Dig, he says, was the first perfectionist I met. He insisted on everything being exactly right and made me use my eyes, no meter reading. He also broadened my tastes, especially with music. This urge for perfection, he laments, causes a lot of problems and takes a lot of emotional effort and expense. You have to work with people who feel like you. So many now say, 'It'll do.' They disregard perfection.

Digby taught him the techniques, but Brian tired of photographing debs, weddings and babies. He heard Michael Forlong lecturing on film to a group of architects and asked him for a job at the National Film Unit. There he was influenced by Forlong, Randall Jarrett, Bert Bridgeman, John Fenny and Margaret Thompson. His film *Snowline Is the Boundary* upset the tourist officials because they felt there was not enough snow in it and too much setting of skis to music. It won awards, but the attitude of the bureaucrats helped drive him out into the world.

Being prepared to live with his subjects, always seeking the emotional moment, made him one of the most renowned of all still photographers. There was a price to pay for his efforts. My style did create a moral problem, he admits, particularly in Arab countries, where they have the Muslim dislike of photographic reproduction of the human figure. I had a difficult experience in a house for the dead in Calcutta. People were brought off the streets to die, and I was intruding on their last minutes. You can only justify that by taking great photographs.

Brian worked his butt off to get great pictures. Ironically, he hates being photographed himself. Like Cartier-Bresson. Henri, he says, feels his work is a private relationship between him and his subject. If you are a photographer, you are committed to express what you see.

With the decline and often demise of the great photo-journals like *Life* (revived in the '70s, only to close this year, 2000) and *Paris Match*, Brian had to find another outlet for his commitment and returned to documentary film-making. Same standards of perfectionism, working intuitively, spontaneously, incessantly.

When I made the Indonesian ballet film, he says, I wanted to try and say something about the ballet. So we got the dancers off the stage and had them tell the ballet story in its original locations. I also made the camera a dancer. I had Grant Foster from the National Film Unit run among the dancers with the hand-held camera, so that it could float with their slow-motion style.

Brake's abiding interest, if not obsession, is Asia. He did a photographic report on the Japanese cinema industry. He was the only photographer to cover China's 10th anniversary celebrations, the first to photograph the Egyptian tombs and much of South-East Asia, most particularly Indonesia and Thailand. He was struck by the similarity of the 4000-year-old Ban Chieng pottery of Northern Thailand to Maori artifacts, as he had these priceless pots transported under machine-gun escort to the ruins they originally came from, so he could photograph them in their natural setting.

Not surprisingly, he laments the passing of still photography from the photo-journals into the art galleries, but he sees no reason why that should be a sentence of museum death. Art galleries, he says, do not have to be static. He knows many in Europe, America and Asia which are alive and encouraging the growth of still photography. He feels there is a need for some structure to shake photographers here out of the salon or pictorial approach, which he freely admits to having for many years himself. He hopes to do something about it, based on Cartier-Bresson's selection of 360 photographs in five sets, one of which he hopes can be purchased by an institution or person here. He sees it as the basis for a centre of photography set up to preserve photographic archives and build a local and international collection, with workshops, lectures, schools and tours. He had his own films and stills on show, he lectures here, and he is preparing large books on Polynesian and Melanesian art. When he has any time, he will build on his section at Titirangi, as any Kiwi would. This is his land, and nobody has shown it better.

Castle the Kiwi
Cultural Alchemist

Ronald Castle was much more than our last Victorian chemist. Not only did he maintain his Devonshire father's business in the melting-pot of the inner Wellington suburb of Newtown, he also maintained everything his father brought with him, and with his sister Zillah added immeasurably to the family tradition of collecting bottles, musical instruments, china, books, dolls, whatever. The Castles filled three tumbledown wooden structures from cellars to attics with an astonishing collectors' cornucopia of international standing. Their problem was, they could not give it away to an indifferent State. No question, in a nation of poozlers, they were our poozlers par excellence. With Zillah recently following Ronald to the hereafter, their internationally significant collection is in danger of being poozled away.

Castle the Chemist of 139 Riddiford Street is still recognisably in the year 2000 the last Victorian pharmacy in the country, now under new ownership. Upstairs in the 1980s, before he moved on to the great alchemical reaction in the sky, Ronald maintained much more than the token reliquary of large, coloured-glass jars and racks of gleaming wood trays below.

They came to us for the cover of the Pharmaceutical Society's centennial book, says a quietly proud Ronald, the eponymous chemist in his restrained tweed jacket and mute blue tie, thick, square, rimless glasses, wispy white hair. The distinctive character of this mild, thin, soft-spoken elderly man is the intense focus he applies to everything, the habit of a professional lifetime measured out in minute healing doses of homeopathic poisons. You know, he says, we have maintained the only Victorian pharmaceutical collection in the country. Everybody else threw out their relics after the war.

Collection seems too modest a word for the museum above his wooden clapboard shop. Here, surely, is pharmacopeiac paradise. We are in a Spielbergian forest of giant carboys full of curiously coloured fluid – pinks, purples, blues, magentas, sulphurous yellows. Wide wooden trays are choked with twisted old barks, leaves and roots that could have been useful for Macbeth's witches. Clusters of bottles and unjolly jars contain the rainbow nostrums, remedies, unctions, ointments, pills, potions, placebos and panaceas that Rawleigh's men can only dream of, all identified by copperplate Latinate nomenclature probably not spoken, even in university Latin classes, in a century.

Iodine for red, Ronald enumerates on fingers as white and spectral as Vincent Price in Edgar Allan Poe mode. Iron perchloride for gold. Copper sulphate for blue. Cobalt for green. All the colours stable for a century now. Modern dyes would have long since faded. The word 'carboy' is of course Persian for bottles used in alchemy, from which chemistry developed. The roots, leaves and barks are the *Materia Medici* set, used for training students. We have here all the developmental stages from alchemy to chemistry.

Ronald's more solid sister Zillah leans across him like a harbour ferry crossing a match-racing yacht. Our family were always collectors, she confides in the same intimate family voice, hushed in the presence of mysterious beauty. One brother collected books, another musical instruments, a sister china.

Sad thing is, Ronald says sadly, we made our wills leaving the pharmaceutical and music collections to the nation. But Parliament passed an act last year preventing the Historic Places Trust from maintaining chattels. So we had to change our will. The pharmaceutical collection goes to the Pharmaceutical Society, the music collection has to be sold off. We appealed to the Minister, but he said the present state of Parliament made this anomaly unlikely to be overturned.

This remains a potential national disgrace, unless some organisation or individual responds to the codicil in their will allowing retention of the collections if someone will maintain them. Two decades later (Zillah recently passed on) the collection is not maintained as its creators intended, with the various parties not agreeing.

Back to Ronald in 1982, the collection in his professionally careful hands, practised at its maintenance since his after-school job of wiping the glass labels on those glowing kauri cabinet trays below. Ronald was the last of seven children, following two brothers and two sisters into the pharmacy, which at its peak had five shops in the capital.

It was chemistry on both sides of the family. Ronald's father John came out from Devon having worked in an English chemist's shop and met Richard Ayres, one of the first apothecaries and botanic chemists in the capital. John Castle married Anne Ayres, the eldest daughter, then passed his pharmacy exams here. In 1888 he set up the Riddiford Street shop and the dynasty began. John Castle went on to become an independent city councillor and president of the Society of Chemists. When he died in 1903, the *Free Lance* magazine praised his caution, enterprise and Devonian courage.

Ronald says little has changed on the outside of the Riddiford Street shop, except they lost the gold-leaf wooden mortar and pestle to the Wahine storm. All five children trained at their father's mighty mortar and pestle now taking pride of place in the museum window above. Wedgwood, Ronald says, inviting me to feel its smooth, heavy texture. Chemists who came out from England for the centenary were fascinated to see this survivor.

I ask about the old whicker basket. That was for weighing infants, Zillah says. My sisters' Mona, who ran the Ascot Pharmacy in Newtown, and Mavis, who ran the Cambridge Terrace one in the city, also ran the first free baby service here. Truby King was often in to see their work.

Those glass jars nearby, Ronald indicates. They contained arrowroot. It was considered good for infants.

The jars look big enough to accommodate infants. You would not know with the opaque white one emblazoned with the imperial coat of arms in rich gold, blue and red. Could the gold leaf have been picked off the others in order to check for infants within? Whatever, one of these jars recently fetched $800 at auction. Americans, Ronald said with a slight hardening of his soft voice, are always coming in making extravagant offers. They can't understand why we won't accept their dollars.

The Americans do not bid for the less obvious memorabilia, like the hand weights with spring connections Eugene Sandow developed into the science of isometrics, making him the world's strongest man and beginning the beefcake boom.

Those two metal racks riddled with holes like grey gruyere? Ah, the cachet or seal for enclosing nasty tastes like quinine in nice wafers. That metal comb sliced up the pill pastry, before it was rolled into pills on that small bowl.

That toy-sized pan? For melting the cocoa butter, for the suppositories. The metal pipette was an homogeniser, another nasty-inside-nice, cod liver oil with emulsifiers to make a viscous white fluid, like Lane's Emulsion.

Chemists, he adds, no longer need such crafts. Factories do all the work.

See this? You'll never guess.

It is a metal clamp. I give in.

It's for thinning corks, says Ronald with just a twitch of

glee. To fit bottles. Now everything's plastic.

I glance at the ear-pourer, but I'd rather not know; it looks like something Hamlet's uncle might have employed. The odd pot there? A still. That chunky metal comb, an electric ray fitted with an early version of a torch battery, used to massage the scalp. Maybe remove it too? Perhaps.

From a corner of the window Ronald recovers his own first bible, *100 Harmless Scientific and Chemical Experiments for Boys*. Yes, he sighs, eyes glinting behind the bifocals. How to blow yourself up in 100 easy lessons.

We look over the ancient apothecary scales that measured in drachms, scruples and grains. The ornate adding-machine toting up pounds, shillings and pence, with plastic metric covers so it is still in use. There are suppository moulds, earthenware water filters, earthenware foot-warmers, triangular counting trays for pills, sealing wax and Irish twine, test tubes and beakers, a German powder slide, a blue Delft ointment jar, blue glass eye-baths. Rows of those little glass bottles now popular as herb containers. His have their Latin tags and range in size from the half-gallon to the thimble.

People still come in for these homeopathic remedies, he says, even though I am retired. Like this baptisia, from the wild indigo root, for a laxative and a mouth wash. Not both at the same time? No. 'Honoured by commands from the Queen and Empress of Russia' is the testimonial on the side. Others were cetaceum, gentian, quassia, cera alba, sassafras – that was for nits in the hair.

Lots of ingredients, says Ronald, were the old approach. We called them shotgun mixtures. If they didn't cure one thing, they cured another.

The favourite is lung balsam, says Zillah. Horehound, liquorice, tincture of ginger, molasses, spirit of orange, aniseed, chloroform.

Yes, says Ronald. Eighteen ingredients. We still have

the cauldron out back

And lots more. A banana-shaped glass baby bottle with tube and teat at one end, air valve at the other, Allenbury's feeder, 1715. Nearby a Heath Robinson metal clamp on a stick with a lever at the other end, for reclaiming objects from the shop window. More bottles in many colours – Dinneford's magnesia, Clement's tonic, Bonnington's Irish Moss.

An 1890s photograph of Castle's shows the massive carbide lamp to complement the gas and Edison filaments. A bellows camera indicates what was used, and developed on the premises, with stereoscopic views and portraits, including one of King Dick, the lion from the zoo. This was established by their father and Dr Crewes, who had rooms up here. The doctor was of religion, a Methodist minister who taught botany, astronomy and phrenology, the study of the meaning of bumps on the skull. Zillah fondly remembers him taking her on his shoulders to feed the sea lions. Dr Crewes was the only person prepared to reach in and stroke King Dick. When Scott and Amundsen were in town, father and Dr Crewes, she recalls, ordered penguins from them for the zoo.

So much to marvel at. An old fountain douche, an obsolete spring truss, coloured prints of the drug trade routes, the benign drugs, that is. Scores of packets and bottles, like Warner's liver pills, Carlsbad salts, Army No. 9 pills for stomach, liver and bowel problems, Little liver pills, Congreve's balsamic elixir for constipation, asthma, coughs, colds, whooping cough, one of the shotgun variety. Vegetable pills for energy, Ashton and Parson's worm cure, fumigating ribbon to scent away epidemics, old prescription books that include remedies such as one powder in a pint of thin, warm gruel, for Mrs Daly's cow.

Now, come around the corner to where the Castles keep

their music, doll and porcelain collections in Colombo Street, viewing by appointment. The music collection is one of the finest in the world, including only one of two complete Bach manuscript holdings, an 8th century Welsh harp, all manner of harpsichords and violins.

This little harp, says Zillah, is Irish, John Egan, about 1820, the Queen's beasts at its base. The big harp is English, same period, Erard. Always had rams' heads at the top.

From one of the Wakefields, says Ronald. They had it in the attic, strung with badminton strings.

Not as bad as the Irish one, Zillah laughs. It was covered in white paint. Given to us by a chap who saw us browsing in a Petone music shop. He used to play it in a touring Australian band. At each venue they had to repaint their instruments to match the decor.

The harps stand upright as a backing for over 40 violins, plus violas, cellos, double-basses, organs, pianos, flutes, clarinets, drums, a sackbut, a yang-gin, an arghool, a kissar, an antique musical smorgasbord. Flanked by glass cabinets bulging with dolls and figurines, er, dolled up to the 18th and 19th centuries' nines.

We bring out the dolls and figurines, says Zillah, when we give talks to young people. It helps them understand how the instruments were used. The hurdy-gurdy, for instance, which was Marie Antoinette's favourite. She played it at Versailles dressed as a shepherdess. The male figurine there in coat and knee-britches is in the mode of the time.

The dolls range far and wide. Shirley Temple, a Maori girl in demure flax regalia, French and English dolls from last century, a troika of soldier boys with side drums, a grumpy-looking kewpie doll over 80 years old. Yes, sighs Zillah, an American woman was here trying to acquire it.

The National Museum, she adds, borrowed some. Te Papa, the new National Museum, might be interested in others, for the Castle Collection has the full representation from the very old bisque to composition to modern plastic, Spanish dancers, Amy Johnson, the Quinn quintuplets, Hummel dolls created by an American nun, Beatrix Potter characters, all of them, a Jane Austen-era doll's house full of Limoges china furniture.

In the glass cabinets are many china sets, of pheasant kitchenware, baleeq Irish china, Coalport, Staffordshire and Rockingham chinaware. The Chinese figurines include a Madonna and Child with baby Jesus bobbing in a hollow china strawberry. One cabinet has the Commemoration china sister Mavis collected, says Zillah, of poor old Edward VIII. Another cabinet displays Victorian souvenir ashtrays, vases, cups, salt cellars, and teapots of Vienna and Wairoa, Manawatu Gorge and Buckingham Palace.

There are tin toy collections of omnibuses, cars, dolls and ships. A Victorian moving picturebook shows girls learning to wash and iron. Dean's Roly Poly rag book unfolds a farmyard scene. A Trigonette puzzle map of the Boer War. Ronald demonstrates a jumping jack, a monkey bobbing up and down on a pole. Zillah explains the skills needed to twirl a Diabolo dumbbell. Coonieflap has grinning clown faces with mouths agape to receive the throw of wooden dice. Pollock's 1887 toy theatre features Aladdin and Punch and Judy. A bunny clock on the wall ticks and tocks big eyes across the room.

The paintings include a Waghorn of Shag Rock near Moa Point in Wellington, Mervyn Taylor engravings, local scenes by Nugent Welch, Sydney Higgs, Beatrice Partridge and nephew John Castle. Flower paintings like Myrtle McDonald's tree tulips, Vera Short's miniatures on ivory. George Chance photographs rich as oil paintings.

Then there are the collections of *Chums* and *Boys Own Paper*, the shells, the old marble clocks, the Rose window rescued from the Methodist Mission in Webb Street.

In this museum, says Ronald, you can touch whatever you like.

And you can hear the instruments played. Ronald fingers a 1609 Stanesby tenor recorder, the Stradivarius, says Zillah, of 17th-century woodwind. Today's equivalents are bright but do not have its bloom.

With that, the student who scored the highest marks recorded at the London School of Music flips a baby violin to her chin and saws a sprightly tune. Bow and violin measure less than 41 centimetres, known as pochette, French for pocket, where they fitted when the dancing master was not instructing in their use. The Castles have a Hogarth depiction of one as part of 'The Rake's Progress'. It is rare to find a pochette, let alone in working order and being worked. They waited 10 years for a London agent to find them one. Zillah was to play it on television, but the studio lights melted the bow. She used a viola bow as a substitute.

Her pupils help. The pan flute made famous by Zamfir is represented by one a pupil, Lucien Rizos of the NZ Symphony Orchestra, brought back from Rumania.

Nearby is a tiny organ that was carried on horseback to colonial church services, a Jewish ramshorn soaked in vinegar and played on days of atonement, a lanky lute my height and known as a buzzing plank or nun's fiddle, the square-stringed crwth, instrument of Druids, for which Zillah regrets there is so little music written.

The music library, says Ronald, was partly developed as a way to learn how to play the instruments, like the 1666 British Museum copy of rather risqué Elizabethan music, for the cithern. We adapted grandfather's turnip watch key for tuning it.

Their love of music was developed at Donald McLean Methodist church, where mother played the organ and their parents sang duets. Then there were the sea shanties their father brought back from a stint in the navy. 'Jack's at home at sea,' Zillah trills. 'Braving storms and dangers.'

The Castles have 500 or so instruments, double that in

books and manuscripts. Many are linked to early settlement here, like the John Broadwood piano that came out on a sailing ship; the first harpsichord to come here, a 1781 Kirkmann with raven wing quills in the stops, similar to the one in the Queen's music room; a Francis Clough square piano *circa* 1850, rescued from a Wellington home; a French organ played at Gabriel's Gully where our gold-rushes began; a spotted kauri double violin case made locally; a Scottish dulcimer brought out by a Salvation Army couple.

The books include the only complete Bach transcriptions here, a lot of Purcell and Handel, the earliest known illustration of solfa, dated 1599, a James Cook illustration of part of a voyage. There are 78 record collections of Melba, Caruso and other early recording stars. The Groves Dictionary of Music has called this the largest collection in Oceania. It may be unique as a living, breathing, wheezing museum. There will not be another pioneer collection to match it. Without government contribution or a private benefactor, it will begin to scatter now to the 21st century winds.

Amazing how long it survived, given the complete absence of security. A burglar, Ronald says, broke in, but didn't take anything. He was probably looking for money, or stereos.

Ronald published five collections of his verse, titles such as 'Arcadian Grove' and 'Psaltery and Trumpet'. From the end poem in his last collection, 'A Farewell in Verse', he writes:

What odours sweet the druggist's store
Emits, what faint nostalgic scent?
What shades protect the ancient lore
In this galenic monument.

If you are curious, Galen was a jocular reference to a physician who made remedies of vegetable, not synthetic, components. In the nation's new synthetic storehouse you might think there would be welcome room for such a potent collection of our shared past and indeed in many significant areas the rest of the world's culture. We should be so lucky.

The Creator of Our New Cuisine and Culture

Harry Seresin was a young Jew who fled here from the Nazis. Appalled to find none of the good things he had left behind, he introduced New Zealanders to coffee culture, to new kinds of cuisine, to wine with food, to professional theatre. Other refugees like Fred Turnovsky and Denis Adam were highly successful businessmen. Harry left business success to his father and his children. He didn't even bother to take friends' advice to buy the land on which he established the restaurant and gallery The Settlement, missing out on millions in the boom in Central Wellington land values. All Harry wanted to do was to talk. He was a magnet for all manner of civilising developments: Graham Kerr taking his cooking to the world, the likes of Ian Mune and Peter Bland and his son Michael translating the talk into professional theatre and film-making all over New Zealand and around the world. Harry just kept talking.

H arry Seresin, sixty-something, tanned, amused, slipped a brick under the broken leg of the wooden stool outside his Settlement Restaurant in central Wellington.

Seems to be the way things are going, he said with a shrug. I'm told a big company is buying the land when the lease expires. My lease requires me to restore it to the way it was.

In 1972 he found an old concrete shed used by a photo-engraver and a clapped-out, clapboard, 90-year-old, two-storey, wooden shop. He hired Christchurch architect Peter Beaven to link them up. Many Oregon beams and recycled Miramar gasworks bricks later, Harry opened up the capital's second real taste of Continental cuisine and culture. Ever since it has been the city's liveliest fusion of old and new music, original pottery and painting, coffee and spicy apple pie and Danish chef Herluf Anderson's ways with steak, fish and chicken.

It teemed like a Dickensian scene with the exhibition or book-launch crowds hanging off the balconies and spilling down the stairs, gathered round Harry at his grand piano playing classical or Russian and German folk songs, or Kurt Wiel, Galya Marder on accordion, NZ Symphony Orchestra members on violin or cello, the bearded Dr Erich Geiringer testing the laws of censorship with some shocking pronouncement, maybe one of those happenings where every trendy, liberal, arty-farty, Ngati karate yuppie and student in town packed the place to bursting, while actors like Tim Eliott, Martyn Sanderson and Barbara Ewing performed spontaneously. Those who cared to could check their gear in the huge mirror of the Larnach Castle sideboard behind the piano. The gas lamps in a row either side of it never went out, fitting for a place that scarcely closed, despite the bureaucratic rules about wining and dining only between certain constrained hours.

Harry was diminutive, but that did not mean he was puny. One of his proudest stories was how he was being bullied by a Nazi at school and told his father. His father showed him a few boxing moves. Next day he planted one on the Nazi's nose, and he fell down in a blubbering heap. Just as well Harry got out of the place.

His father insisted. He had already got out of Russia just ahead of the same sort of trouble, so he knew the signs. Two drunken Cossacks had grabbed him off the street and prodded him against the wall with their rifles, demanding if this filthy Jew who had no honest working-man's dirt under his fingernails could give any reason why such a leech should not be shot. Harry's father said they should see inside his head, there it was as filthy as any working man's fingernails. The Cossacks roared with laughter, told him to make himself scarce before they changed their minds. He did, leaving behind a fortune. He made another in Germany, left that, finally made a third fortune in England.

I once saw Harry's fortitude at the Settlement, when he arrived late to receive complaints about the behaviour in the private room. It had been hired for an after-Test function and was full of Lions and All Blacks. Harry strode up to the curtain, flung it aside to the sight of large men standing on the dining trestles with their trousers around their ankles, mooning for the flashbulbs of young women amid drunken shouts of encouragement. Harry, half the height of these heroes, told them to get out. Two very well-known All Blacks rushed for the side exit, slipping in the grease-trap in their hurry. The Lions lads were not far behind. Later the be-kilted Lions lock Gordon Brown returned to apologise for the behaviour of his colleagues. Harry invited him to sit down for a drink.

Harry was vastly experienced at handling all sorts of revellers. He was, after all, the man who gave Wellington, and indeed New Zealand, its first taste of his then subversive mix of culture and coffee when he opened the Coffee Gallery above Roy Parson's bookstore in Massey House in 1958. Per his usual non-business sense, he settled for the mezzanine floor of the first high-rise office building. He had discussed its design with another of his refugee compatriots, Ernst Plischke, who eventually returned after the war to professorial status in Vienna. During the Coffee Gallery's decade-long run it introduced New Zealanders to real coffee and such exotic food as Harry's mother's goulash. It was also the gathering place for every budding and blossoming poet and painter and performing flea in a city starved of such a venue. We trainee teachers spent as much time as possible there, listening to beatnik poets and chatting each other up.

The Coffee Gallery could not provide the complete performing context actors were demanding. The actors Martyn Sanderson, Tim Eliott and Peter Bland told Harry they needed a theatre. They told him again back at his place above Oriental Bay, the last town acre left, with mature macrocarpas and a magnificent lounge in whose fireplace Harry burned the macrocarpa limbs blown off by the high winds. There he invited continuous company. All those not totally committed to rugby, racing and beer brought bottles of wine and ate the kind of tucker not troubled with Edmond's cookbook entries, like olives and garlic sausages and smelly cheeses and French bread and *marron glacé* and many other things brought along from the Dixon Deli, likely as not by its proprietor, another of Harry's refugee *confrères*, Martin Chait. Harry had the effortless ability to both talk and put all at their ease, no matter how young and keen and gauche, and at the same time more likely than not he was tapping out tunes on his grand. Sure, he told the eager-beaver young wannabe professional actors, let's do it, let's introduce food and wine and theatre downtown.

Really, it was as natural as breathing to Harry. When he had arrived here still in his teens in 1938, he didn't try to fit in to this cultural outpost. For years I heard him denouncing the warrior culture of the All Blacks, but one day in an unguarded moment he admitted to the thrill of scoring a rugby try at his English school. He also admitted to being a Zionist, albeit an armchair one – unless some Philistine sportsfolk invaded his space. He was a young man in a sporty culture he could care less about, so he went searching and found the French Club, where he met a lifelong friend, young journalist Erik de Mauny, who became a distinguished BBC foreign correspondent. They boarded in Oriental Bay, below his house now. In those days writers, painters, musicians and foreigners congregated in a house nearby in Macfarlane Street. One day there the promising painter

Peter McIntyre told Harry he looked like a Lithuanian yak. People laughed and kept laughing. Peter said he didn't think it that funny. But it was, said Harry. I am Lithuanian.

Harry was no painter or poet, but he was an innovator. He imported a pizza-making machine. It was a disaster. Kiwis didn't want this foreign muck. So he went to music classes. He brought back to his flat these painters, poets and foreigners for coffee and cognac. He started importing 'strange' pottery and Scandinavian furniture in the 1950s, making sufficient money to buy this old place up the hill. It was big enough to fit in all the painters, poets and foreigners who wanted to call for a coffee and cognac. Likely lads, young Milan Mrkusich a promising painter, Steve Jelicich of Jasmad Architects, Ernst Plischke, who asked Harry what he could do with the shop-window of the new Massey House he had just designed for the Meat and Dairy Boards. Harry knew. Ernst told him the primary produce clients wanted something prestigious, like selling cars or airline tickets. Ernst liked Harry's idea better, so Harry got in 10 good years of coffee culture, before the owners trebled the rent.

It seemed the right time to invite these three actors up to his house, along with the likes of Bruce Mason, a playwright in search of a theatre, academic enthusiasts like John Roberts, Don McKenzie, Roger Savage. Many attempts had been made to get professional theatre off the ground. But Harry had heard about the old Walkabout Restaurant up for grabs. He grabbed it. It was a fully equipped restaurant, says Harry, so we decided on a theatre restaurant.

On 20 November 1964 Edward Albee's *The Zoo Story* opened, starring Martyn Sanderson and Peter Bland. A young ex-Flight Lieutenant chef called Graham Kerr flared crepe suzettes for those up front, and Harry's wife, Helen, cooked Swedish meatballs and rice for the other 50 or so.

There were glasses of oil floating in wicks at the tables, Harry's preference to the usual candles dripping down empty Mateus Rosé wine bottles. The oil worked until a waitress tripped and oil went everywhere, and so did the patrons. Downstage was away laughing.

Bruce Mason, as local newspaper theatre reviewer, said it was the most promising omen in New Zealand theatre in years with utterly right ambience, lots of chat and sherry and meatballs and pancakes. Patrons agreed, packing the place out for a Victorian melodrama. There were late shows, Barry Crump spinning yarns, Treena Kerr doing instant revue, Erich Geiringer reciting Eskimo Nell. Harry was treasurer, with lots of bills. Everybody went off for the Christmas holidays. The place wound down.

Harry revived things the next year by suggesting Bland write a play about being in bed, which we all did. Bland delivered; a young Ian Mune was in the cast. Then Bruce Mason did his one-man show, Tim Eliott another, Richard Campion directed *Oh, What a Lovely War*, Graham Kerr organised fundraising to improve the theatre.

Most of the income came from the food. Harry said that made the difference between Downstage and the local amateur theatres. The food was the only way, he says, we could afford to put on the theatre. Without the theatre, no crowds; without the food no money from the crowds to pay for professional theatre. And without professional theatre no way would those late-night satirical shows have run on and on, spawning new talent like John Clarke, Ginette McDonald, Paul Holmes, John Banas. In this theatre Lyn of Tawa was born and nurtured, with encouragement from Bruce Mason and Roger Hall in the wings.

Harry used his coffee-bar staff. David Morris brought in food but became so successful he moved to Auckland, Australia, the world. Harry took on his usual eclectic mix, including a Siberian lass who spoke no English and whom he just prevented from serving offal and vegetable scraps to the party of the Downstage benefactress Sheilah Winn. Worse was the night the chef collapsed drunk. Harry and actor/writer Jonathan Hardy cooked a paella.

Every opening night Harry had to apply for a liquor licence. Thus began the theatre licence in New Zealand, which extended to opera, ballet and any live performance. The inspectors expected beer and were not happy about wine. Even worse was the vodka the night Chekhov opened, with piroshki and borscht prepared by cooks Harry requested from the Russian Embassy. When a play opened based on Tuhoi legends, Harry got Ngati Poneke to cook up Maori bread, pork and puha, muttonbirds.

Thanks to the innovative food offerings, enough money was made to sponsor 41 professional productions in the first two years. Downstage was over the hump on which other efforts around New Zealand had foundered. Public and corporate donations kept the theatre going, its graduates moving about – Eliott to Australia, Bland to London, the Kerrs to everywhere, Roger Hall to Dunedin, Pat Evison to Australia, Barbara Ewing to England.

And Harry, his job done, moved across town to found the Settlement Restaurant, where music and poetry and pots and paintings were served with the food. It was quite a fusion, even unto the tables, old oak bases Harry got for a song, with rimu tops added. He bought the piano from a regular there, Colleen Rae Gerrard, that sideboard from Larnach Castle, organ, gas lamps, a resident potter Ian McClymont out back with maybe his wife Anne Flannery performing out front. The vaulting chapelesque connecting room was good acoustically, encouraging Harry's first love, music. He had small Mozart operas performed there, 18th century lute music, rock music from Blerta and Arrdvark, sitar, gamelan, jazz, Russian, Czech, Hungarian, Austrian, Japanese, German, a Chilean refugee on guitar.

A Puckish fellow, Harry liked the conflict of chamber music and eating, which held up meals because the performers wanted quiet. Harry lost money on that. Undaunted, he put on old poets like Denis Glover and new poets like Sam Hunt, book launchings for Tony Simpson and Jim Siers, exhibitions of established painters like John Drawbridge and new painters like Gary Tricker, jewellers, leathermakers, weavers, herbalists, Warwick Teague's aluminium ice-cream cones; the Japanese ambassador liked them.

Downstairs diplomats, Rotarians, bureaucrats and academics ate steaks and veg that were not overcooked, seafood and smoked eel for the more adventurous. Upstairs anything went, like Yugoslav bagpipes, a woman cleaving a gallon can of tomato puree.

Harry had overspent on the renovations, and it took seven years to pay them off. He was commended by the council and food writers. Of course, he wasn't making money. He did too much, put on too many things at his own cost. But he was also thinking that now this was established, it was time to try something new. He sold the restaurant to his staff, began his plans to do something with disused wharf buildings. And still all those poets, painters and foreigners flocked to Harry's home, to talk about the possibilities of life. Have we ever had quite such an innovator in our Kiwi lives?

The Long, Literary, Loving Recorders of Our Kiwi Memory

The Manson family have over two generations recorded more of the history of New Zealand than anybody else. It began in World War Two London with Celia Manson writing stories about her pioneering New Zealand family and expanded back here into long-running newspaper columns and many books of New Zealand history, extended by her son Hugo co-founding the New Zealand Oral History Archive. His father Cecil's love of France led to the Mansons setting up the Katherine Mansfield Fellowship at Menton, furthering the Manson contribution to the literary stimulation of this country. The Mansons made a major contribution to New Zealand's memory bank.

Celia Manson poured the milk. Cecil Manson poured the tea. Afternoon sun streams across the white veranda, glints off brasswork, buffs up polished furniture, bounces off the ribbed surface of the silver sugar bowl that was a wedding present from her parents and settles softly over the sitting room of their Day's Bay home. Around them are rich old landscapes and a gold statuette from Paris of a woman rampant, as well as Cecil's own large, bright oils, abstracts, nudes, landscapes, one of them an island and lighthouse hovering in a mazy blue expanse of ocean and sky. The bookcases behind them are full of their books and other New Zealand works; the table is piled up with research papers. The ambience is of leisurely scholarship, half a century of elegant and industrious labour in their white wooden bungalow, a stone's throw from Katherine Mansfield's house at the Bay.

My first writing, says Cecil, adjusting his hearing aid, was just after World War One. I went out to Jerusalem as a reporter and sales manager for father's *Egyptian Gazette*, which is still the English paper there but run by Egyptians now. Money was pouring into Egypt then, before there was any conflict in the area, and it was decided to expand the paper to Palestine. There wasn't much else for me to do – I was only 19; I wasn't trained at anything.

Celia is having none of Cecil's English understatement. You know, she says, fondly grasping his arm, Cecil was a company commander at Gallipoli before he was 19.

Orrhhh! says Cecil, waving a dismissive hand. There was only a quarter of us left. We got the rank because the others were not there. Anyway, Sir Ronald Storrs, the Governor of Jerusalem, put me forward for a *Daily Mail* correspondent there. I got five pounds a cable recording the beginning of the Arab/Jewish troubles, when the Arabs were being pushed off their land.

Cecil, you know, Celia intervenes, used to sing duets at the Governor's parties.

Orhh! Cecil objects. I was trying to learn singing at the time.

You had a lovely voice, dear.

Cecil's voice is silent.

That painting of the island and lighthouse? It's like a blue Turner.

Ahh, yes, Cecil concedes. Turner is a favourite of mine. Celia gave me a book of his reproductions for Christmas.

Cecil has untamed, long, white hair, a trim white goatee, an open-necked white shirt, a slightly abstracted look behind thick glasses. He is the very image of an impressionist painter. When he wears his straw hat to water the garden, the image is complete.

Celia is delicate, soft-spoken, a very attractive and determined woman who most of her life has been what she

186

always wanted to be, an author. She is so proud of Cecil, who took up painting late and has exhibited in London and Paris. They have been engaged in a loving literary duet through their marriage, four decades co-authoring eight historic works, several children's books and countless articles and broadcasts.

Cecil is 86, and Celia is as proud as punch of the new cooking he is experimenting with. They like new things, even though they are distinguished for their evocation of the old. Perhaps this is most happily blended in the Katherine Mansfield writing fellowship at Menton they co-founded, where new and exciting, or at the very least promising, and usually young New Zealand writers get their chance to spend a season in the South of France just writing what they wish, absorbing Katherine Mansfield's ambience and history in this glamorous old habitation of hers. The Mansons' two latest books are another example of their synchronicity, both published recently on the same day, her *Widow of Thorndon Quay*, her 12th book, his *A World Away*, his ninth. Hers is the second part of her story of her great-grandmother, his the first half of his memoirs; the books are each dedicated to the other.

Celia's third part to her story of a New Zealand family will be about her mother, a teller of tales to her nine children on winter nights in the original Masterton hospital, which had become their home. Her mother had a gift for mimicry, especially with Irish accents, and Celia says she inspired her to write.

At first Celia wrote children's stories, some appearing in the *Weekly News*. An aunt's bequest bankrolled her OE. She travelled to London, where she met a local, Cecil Manson.

Cecil had gone off journalism after a blocking incident. He had gone in the company of Kim Philby's father to the Dead Sea, to interview King Hussein. He got there to find he had no questions to ask.

He switched in London to the salted codfish business and did fashion drawings for the *Observer* and *The Times* and a host of other new things which you can read about in his delightfully offhand memoirs. He makes even the experience of being under fire at Gallipoli sound like a cross between a *Chums* or *Boys Own* yarn and a Sunday stroll on the beach. Then he flew over the battlefield, his first plane flight, ending as a perilous pea rattling around inside a bullet-ridden sieve.

His memoirs end with the beginning of their long and loving relationship and an anecdote told with great gusto about a man in his 80s who had lost his partner of half a century who had fed and bed him well but 'some'ow I never took to the woman'. Not so in his own case, not by a circuit of the globe.

The Mansons had son Hugo in 1941 and son Bill a few years later. Celia was feeling that characteristic homesickness that afflicts us Kiwis, even in our cultural Mecca. She transformed it into a radio series for the BBC, for which she was already presenting broadcasts about the life of a housewife in war-torn London. The dramatised series has become her two books on the history of a New Zealand family. Back then she relied on her memories of her mum's stories.

She travelled to Bristol to do the series. The Queen Mother was living nearby and came to see one of them produced. I was worried, Celia recalls, her seeing me pregnant and asking why I wasn't at home looking after the baby.

Just as well she wasn't. Cecil had had enough of sitting in Supreme HQ in North London watching bombs raining down on his family in South London. Cecil admits to being attached to the secret intelligence section doing the D-Day preparations. Rumour hath it he was one of the Enigma code-breakers. He would cycle back from Bushy Park not able to say anything about his work except that Celia should listen to the news the next day. Being busy with other things, Celia missed the news.

It was strange, she says, because the next day I was out trying to get stories on how people felt about D-Day and there was little excitement. People were just getting on with their daily lives.

Celia got on with something new, a children's book, a chapter a day. *Willow's Point* was published under the name C. Drummond Manson, the middle family name laying claim to the earldom of Perth, a story of Culloden and a lifetime in hiding, which Celia relates at the end of her new book.

Her favourite illustrator, George Soper of *Chums* and *Boys Own Paper*, was dead, so she settled for his daughter Eileen, who did the Enid Blyton covers. She says it sold well in Britain and here because children thought it was an Enid Blyton; clearly she has picked up Cecil's English ways. Both are diffident and self-deprecating, which with their books has the virtue of dramatic understatement.

After the war Cecil ran a photographic studio in Nelson. Celia comes as close as she can to negative criticism when she says he was too much of a perfectionist to make any money.

How the hell, he says with amused wonder, did we ever manage to build a house there?

Wellington was beckoning both of them for broadcasting work, so they moved to Eastbourne and have stayed.

Their first historic book collaboration on the Hokianga came out of a broadcasting research trip. The following year, 1954, they began the historical series 'Before We Forget' in the Saturday *Dominion*. The series ran a decade and yielded three books. I arrived in Wellington in 1960, and it was not long before those Saturday articles were a must-read, inspiring me, I told the Mansons, to write my own newspaper series on local history.

Their collaborations continued in book form on Dr Agnes Bennett, early writing, last year *The Affair of the Wellington Brig*, which there has been talk of filming. Celia's latest, *Widow of Thorndon Quay*, ends with her great-grandmother's death in 1898. She is almost into this century, ready to tap into the raw material of the family scrapbook, in which her brothers and sisters have, at her invitation, written down their memories.

Her father was a headmaster in Masterton. He used to say he couldn't give his large brood much, but he could give them a good education and good teeth. Celia says she hopes her sons become writers. Certainly they have been given the scope for it, being taken by their parents to Aix-en-Provence, where Cecil and Celia honeymooned.

Cecil has always been a francophile and Celia says he won her over. Their lads went to the local lycée once attended by Zola and Cézanne, where Zola won the painting prize, not Cézanne, they add with glee.

Their combined interests in francophilia and developing Kiwi cultural identity were married up in the restoration of KM's Menton cottage. It was a long battle to win official support for their idea, typical perhaps of their Celtic stubbornness in the face of indifferent Establishment types. They both have Scottish ancestors. His come from the Shetlands and Caithness, the name Manson a contraction of the Danish Magnusson. His lot worked their way down the British Isles to Nottingham, where an ancestor found the iodine antidote to goitre, then on to London. Her ancestors in the 'Braveheart' country of Stirling above Glasgow had a fine ancestral home the Mansons visited just before it was bulldozed. Celia asked for the two stained-glass panels entitled Night and Day, one an owl and a bat, the other pigeons and sunrise. These old-world emblems of her origins rest in the window of the sitting-room, filtering the late afternoon sun that belts in across the harbour, flashes across the enclosed veranda clogged with notes of books past and future, splashes against the stained glass and fragments into many coloured flickerings around the sitting-room.

The Mansons have infiltrated their words into the sitting-rooms of our heritage, casting an affectionate light on much of our history. That affection may be at one remove in their books. It is as clear as sunlight in the long duet of their loving lives together.

Their sons are fulfilling their ambitions. Bill and Hugo were known for their television presentations, Bill in more personality mode, Hugo exposing scams on *Fair Go*. Bill is in the States now writing a novel. Hugo has established and contributed in large part to the nation's huge oral memory archive. He says the seed for that was sown at Aix-en-Provence secondary school. French was a major part of his degree, and he returned to the area, struck at how the inhabitants could recite whole local histories going back centuries. He noted how stories often revolved around roads and rivers. Back here he did the pilot oral history about Martinborough, the locals telling stories centred on the road and the river in flood.

Educated in French, with a taste for German beer, it is the old-world connections that prompted Hugo to enlarge on his parents' endeavours with the epic project of recording all the memories Kiwis care to speak into a microphone. The Mansons have done as much as anybody to give this emerging Kiwi culture a memory, the *sine qua non*, as my old Latin teacher would say, for having a culture.

The Great-Granddaughter
of New Zealand

Irma O'Connor spent a very long lifetime demanding a fair go for her grandfather, Edward Gibbon Wakefield. She had some of the mesmeric qualities of her famous ancestor and used them to continuous effect to remind New Zealanders that EGW did not abduct heiresses and establish settlements here to get rich but died here poor, fighting the landed gentry bent on recreating New Zealand in their own advantaged Little Britain image. As mostly Scottish Catholics with our own modest beginnings on the ground floor of New Zealand development, my father and I visited Irma with, I guess, mixed feelings about her famous English ancestor.

Irma O'Connor opened the door of her Auckland flat and gave my father and me the once-over with blue eyes as dense and dazzling as the huge variegated opal cameo brooch she wore.

Two visiting lads, she said, eyes twinkling. Come in, come in.

She directed us with her cane down the passageway, past the gallery of famous relations, none more famous or infamous than the consummate colonial planner and father of New Zealand, Edward Gibbon Wakefield, or EGW as she calls him. My father was obviously still recovering from being lumped in with me as 'lads', but then we were to this little old lady in her mid-nineties. Dad was a mere stripling in his seventies. Miss O'Connor spans this country's life as the last direct living descendant of the man who founded it.

Did you see that activist in the paper? she said scornfully, directing us to easy chairs in the sitting-room, pouring tea.

He said EGW abducted heiresses for their money, established settlements here to get rich quick. Nonsense! He died poor! Help yourselves to cakes before I clear the table.

We lads did as we were told, nibbling coconut macaroons and sipping tea from fine blue china resting on lace doilies on the long, low, gleaming wooden coffee table, or perhaps, tea table. Irma made small talk about the pollen count being so impossibly high in Kohi this year, how much she would give to have that neighbour's privet hedge removed. You might be able to see just beyond it, she said, a tightening in her voice.

We lads dutifully craned over the privet tendrils. I could see pohutukawas, a glimpse of the Hauraki as cloudy blue as Irma's eyes. I glanced sideways at Dad, trying to guess what we were supposed to be looking at. It wasn't something she approved of. I could see the black stone Melanesian Mission School. Was it something about graves? Couldn't be her ancestors, they were all in the city cemetery behind The Terrace by the motorway in Wellington. I had seen her there on her annual pilgrimage to the Wakefield plots, populated with her poor ancestors, she had insisted then, as distinct from the land-grabbing missionaries. Ah hah!

Yes, I said. The Melanesian Mission.

She nodded approval. I had remembered her Wellington lecture. Bishop Selwyn. Was he the one the Aussies called the flogging parson?

Bishop Selwyn founded it in 1859, said Dad, who knows his Auckland history.

Hmphhh! she said.

A good stone's throw, I suggested, hoping to send a coded cliché to Irma without drawing Dad into what could be a tricky discussion. He would no doubt get on to Bishop Pompallier, and I wasn't sure where Irma stood there.

To business, she declared, resolving the situation, beginning the clearing of the table. We helped.

Irma went over to an old oak trunk, waved away our offer to open it for her and took out a parchment. This she unfurled along the table, reaching for a brass ornament to hold it in place. It was too long for the table. She held the partly opened end and told us this was the Wakefield clan back to non-conformist Quaker Roger Wakefield, 1592. As we looked at the copperplate linking ladders of her family tree, Irma told us tales of consistent commitment to conscience, causes and reforming zeal. Cousin Elizabeth Fry promoted prison reform. Grandmother Priscilla Wakefield founded the first savings bank. Dad nodded sagely, having run post office savings banks for years as postmaster in Auckland and the Bay of Plenty. Most worthwhile, he approved.

EGW's problems, she said, directing a cursory nod at the Melanesian Mission, which is now a restaurant, began with the hostility and propaganda spread by the Church of England Missionary Society and its spokesman, Colonial Secretary Lord Glenelg. EGW upset that Establishment with his radical colonisation schemes that ignored the missionary work.

Dad was frowning. I guessed he was looking to work around to the difficulties the Catholics faced. After all, they had to build their own printing press in Russell to publish Maori translations of Catholic doctrine, to counter the anti-Catholic propaganda. But the Quakers were not in his frame. We were fifth generation Aucklanders who had benefited from the colonisation schemes, coming out from no prospects in Scotland to bake and plait rope in Ponsonby and put down pretty good roots. Our gripe had always been with the other missionary sects shutting out the Catholics. Irma, however, was on her lifelong mission to resurrect EGW's good name. What Dad was starting to say about missionaries and the question I was shaping to deflect us away from any potential cross-currents with a reference to family tree research, which Dad was currently engaged in, was all overridden by Irma levering herself up with her cane, again telling us to stay seated, and returning the parchment to the chest.

The story begins, she said firmly over her shoulder, with EGW's alleged gold-digging seductions. He was secretary in the diplomatic service in London when he fell in love with Eliza Pattle. They were both under age, he just 20. They ran off and married in Edinburgh because they knew both families would not sanction the union.

I could see Dad frowning. It was only recently we had discovered a Munro ancestor living a wretched life as a washerwoman with seven children in Edinburgh, straw stone floor, no man, no money, no hope. This Dickensian twaddle about lovers running away. I was getting edgy about bringing Dad along, though he had been interested to meet this living link with all our pasts.

Irma was standing, leaning on her cane, commanding our attention with those mesmeric eyes. They had four happy years before her death, she declared. Here's the proof.

She had a red leather book in her hand. Eliza's diary, she said triumphantly. Listen. She sat herself in the cane-backed easy chair, checked we were paying attention. She opened the diary carefully. Now, she said, this is Eliza: Went out today to please my dear Edward. He is so happy to know that he has made me completely so. Irma's voice quivers. She closes the diary. A typical extract, she says. From the ailing mother of his two children.

I dare not look at Dad. This is not his cup of tea. Manly Kipling for him, not sentimental Dickens tripe.

After Ellen's death, she continues, Edward became an attaché at the embassy in Paris. Our family belief is the abduction of Ellen Turner was in response to a dare from his father's second wife, Frances, whose father lived near the Turners.

I cannot help twitching. I can hear Dad saying PREPOSTEROUS! even though he has not. Why did I ask him along? This will be a ...

Ellen *chose*, Irma emphasises the verb, to go with EGW. They did not consummate the marriage.

I relax. I am sure Dad has too.

A week later at Calais, she continues, Ellen's outraged uncles arrive with a solicitor and a Bow Street Runner.

I know this bit. Dad will approve. He might even start thinking about *The Moonstone* and other early English police stories, on to Sherlock Holmes, away from this scandalous story.

EGW, she is saying, could not be arrested on French soil. But, he returned voluntarily to stand trial, choosing imprisonment rather than a heavy fine that would have disadvantaged his children's settlement from their mother. It's all in here.

She is patting the plain buff dust-jacket of her biography of her grandfather. I slip into the safe territory of questions about the book's origins. It was published in 1928. The publishers Selwyn and Blount asked her to write it as a contribution to the 'Empire Builders' series. They knew of her from articles she had written for newspapers and magazines like *Country Life* and *Field*, when she was a young journalist on her OE visiting Wakefield relations in England in 1925. She had a job with the newly opened New Zealand House in publicity, and she lived in The Strand. She admits she was fortunate interest in New Zealand was high following the visit there of the Duke and Duchess of Kent. She wrote gossip for the tabloids, more formal material for *The Times*. Here she frowns. Eighty reviews of the book, the same steel in her voice we heard when referring to the Mission House. The only unfavourable one was in *The Times*.

She is glaring at us. Dad has no truck with the Anglican

Establishment either, but before he can say anything I ask her why.

The newspaper, she says scornfully, is the mouthpiece of the British Government. They never forgave EGW for founding colonial settlements without their permission. Look!

She is up again and back to the trunk. She extracts a letter, waves it at us. After my book appeared, she says, this letter. From Duncan Campbell Mackenzie. His father was at the legal dinner when Lord Colonsay said EGW's trial was a miscarriage of justice. He had been called to give evidence of Scottish law. He says here, the case was pressed to – I quote – 'render Edward Gibbon Wakefield ineligible as a Member of Parliament'.

Her eyes are flashing like prize opals. You can see why. EGW and his father were standing on a platform of improved conditions for underpaid workers, including those in silk factories. Ellen Turner's father was a wealthy silk manufacturer. To have the wedding annulled he spent 10,000 pounds, a huge sum in those days. Why? Because EGW and his father were a threat to vested interests.

I relax. Dad is a Labour Party man, Peter Fraser a Scotsman. Here is perfidious English political tactics by the Establishment in the era before Churchill. I ask how long her grandfather was in Newgate Prison.

Three years, she says indignantly. There he met and spoke to many youngsters who were choosing transportation to the colonies as an obvious preference to the hangman's rope. EGW developed his famous scheme that resolved the Establishment's perceived problem of the surplus population of Britain's rural poor through transportation without chains, using venture capital to give them work contracts, allowing them eventually to buy a stake in the new land. To achieve this, he wanted a minimum price that would stop the land sharks buying all the land. That, she snaps, was the crux.

That's why Karl Marx criticised him, I propose, knowing that will aid Dad's acceptance of her story. He must be veering towards it anyway, knowing how incensed he gets about transportation of the poor from Britain, especially orphan lads.

They forced his scheme to be a land company, Irma says angrily, to operate commercially, causing EGW to resign in disgust. She waves her hands for emphasis. The New Zealand Company was founded by great men with little pockets; it fell into the hands of little men with great pockets.

That kind of rhetoric is worthy of her grandfather. I ask her if she knew about New Zealand television canning the eight-parter on the Wakefields in the wake, so to speak, of Muldoon's objection to the million dollars spent on EGW's old rival Governor Grey. She is glaring. I quail.

The BBC, she says, to my relief, did a fine programme on EGW, called *The Great Persuader*. The proof was when he came to Wellington despite a stroke, to battle the capitalists who had hijacked his company. He stood for the rural poor in the Hutt Valley. They voted him in to Parliament, where he campaigned to get them the chance of the land he had promised them. He died poor and with little land himself.

Invented the Kiwi philosophy, I suggest, that Jack is as good as his master. And he was the architect of protecting Maori interest by reserving 10 percent of the land for them. His farsightedness you can see in suggesting Maori should be able to present petitions in the Maori tongue. I am gabbling with relief, regurgitating what she told me in Wellington.

Even his most violent political opponent, she says, ignoring my outburst ...

Sorry, I say. Grey? Glare. Not Grey. Who was he?

She glares. As I was about to say, the *New Zealand Spectator*. It acknowledged after his death that his plan

199

brought prosperity to many who would only have known poverty and misery in Britain.

Like our ancestors, I say, turning to Dad.

Yes, he says. Of course, the Labour Party had much to do ...

At the 1940 Centennial, Irma interrupts, I was invited to speak alongside the prime minister and other leaders.

Fraser, another Scotsman, I say ingratiatingly, foolishly, then wonder if he was, or was Savage still alive and still therefore prime minister?

Dad is nodding at Irma.

I told them, she says, smiling, about EGW always buying certain toffees to spread around at meetings, to gum up the objectors when he wanted a motion passed. Walter Nash – he'd run a sweet shop in Birmingham – got up and said he would like the recipe; he was sure it was better than the acid drops he used.

Dad enjoys that, says politely how interesting her comments have been. Irma ends the chat on this sweet note. I think it useful to ask as we leave, for Dad's sake or maybe mine, how much EGW died with. He took, she says at the door, the standard allotment of a town acre and 100 country acres. You should look around the church lands over that way, looking meaningfully back over the privet hedge at the black smudge of the Melanesian Mission House.

We drive back past it, surrounded now by bathers and kids playing in the adjacent park. Dad tells me it was founded because St Johns College up in Meadowbank was too cold for Melanesian students. When they no longer came, the plans for a museum were abandoned because it was too damp. He is content with this contribution. He says nothing about Quakers seducing heiresses, as I thought he might. Maybe he is weighing up EGW. I already have. Most of us Kiwis get a fair crack at EGW's dream of everybody being able to afford a piece of land.

The Pioneering Playwright's
Pursuit of Golden Godzone Weather

Bruce Edward George Mason, the country's Grand Old Playwright, was dying in the sitting-room of his suburban Wellington home. His doctor wife, Diana, was nearby to put a time limit on the endless stream of callers come to pay homage and tax his dwindling strength. Cancer had him by the throat, denying him the splendid voice that launched a thousand performances of his one-man tour de force The End of the Golden Weather. This evocation of his Takapuna childhood is the most moving, hilarious and affecting contribution New Zealand has made to its own and the world's stage. From the cultural fracturing of a Maori family in The Pohutukawa Tree to the lyric agony of The Blood of the Lamb, Mason had a long and mostly lonely career as the country's pioneering playwright in search of Kiwi identity. By the end all his dramatic chooks had come home to roost. Sprawled out and stick-thin behind a clumsy-looking oxygen mask and machine pump, he looked like a defeated Dalek wheezing theatrically, no longer the Antipodean Oscar Wilde delivering Joycean agenbite and much wit.

Not true! He lurched upright, flinging aside this inhibiting prop, croaking out the limitations he saw in my *Listener* article provocatively headed 'Do Pakeha Have a Culture?' His whole life had been taken up with the lack of Kiwi culture, his self-appointed task to chart a century of displacement and fragmentation for Maori as well as Pakeha. Disputatious to the last, eager for intellectual fray, Mason did not go gentle into that good night, but raged against the dying of his busy life.

As happened with many an emerging Kiwi, he was

inspired by old-world performances, in his case Welsh actor Emlyn Williams recreating Welsh poet Dylan Thomas on New Zealand stages. Mason was not inspired to ape the offerings of another marginalised culture, but instead to show New Zealanders that one of us could do as well with local material and in the process exorcise the colonial cultural cringe. Mason spent his professional life dedicated to this task, much of it a splendidly theatrical voice crying in the wilderness, a stage prophet, our first Kiwi thespian voice. We had Kiwi voices in politics and writing, but here was one at last to challenge the deferring theatre audiences who only perceived English vocalists as authentic.

Bruce in the process came across as a Pharisee berating Philistines. In gruff, manly, paternalistic New Zealand, he seemed like an effete snob in a velvet jacket, sneering at yobs who didn't dig Mozart operas. He never compromised with his own elitist tastes. When I was visiting him before he was struck down by cancer, in the early 1980s, he was back from his refresher course in the culture pots of Europe.

Posed as usual in the window of his Kilbirnie sitting-room, Bruce confessed to a good year, writing four commissioned television plays, the first and pretty well the last time the public service television system would indulge such uncommercial frippery. He had celebrated, he said, by going back to Italy. There was something appealing, he drawled, about centuries of culture, continuity with the past, when you came from a country that didn't have one.

The laconic lash, a trademark Mason pose. We lost the clan and family and guidelines in the months voyaging across the sea, he said with a sigh. It is a numbing thing, to be cut off from the past.

The dismissive flap of a limp wrist, a scornful side glance out the window at flat suburbia, the campy gestures he has always flung in the face of indifferent middle New Zealand. I am aware, he drawled, how unwelcome the bearer of bad news is in a society possessed by the notion that you work for somebody else and then you play for yourself. Nosey-parker playwrights can get off the grass – or, in suburbia, the wet concrete.

This may seem a bit defensive several decades on, with Kiwi playwrights sprouting like mushrooms in backstreet vaults of every provincial town in the land. It is still worth noting that nobody among these callow scratchers has yet matched the lyrical passion and aching evocativeness or even the hysterical humour of Mason in full dramatic flight. His wounded refuge in European opera is no longer relevant now European opera has come to us. Nobody much remembers the fight he had on his hands.

His fight, like that of many a Kiwi lad, began refusing to worship on the grim altar of his father's expectations. He was clear about this in a 1978 open letter from Haydn to Mozart, from John the Baptist or Moses who never made the promised land wherein his celebrated successor Roger Hall was flourishing. Bruce was very generous about Roger's success, as he was characteristically with new talent. What he wanted though was to talk to Roger about their fathers. Mason Senior, Bruce confided, never came to his son's plays as a matter of principle. His brother Tim, two years younger, an All Black, was the son on whom his father doted. Bruce confronted his father at the end of his life with the remark that Tim was the son he hoped to be and Bruce was the son he could have been. Bruce to many was vain, but it was honest vanity. A few weeks before the death of Mason *père*, he did go to see *Awatea* with Inia Te Wiata, one of four plays the great Maori opera and stage star had asked Bruce to write. Mason Senior made one comment, that he 'couldn't hear a bloody word'.

Born in Wellington in 1921, Bruce was five when the family moved to Auckland, a few years later to Takapuna. Bruce says it began there, scribbling tell-tale signs in the wet concrete of our expanding suburbia. He actually hid in the flax bush and scribbled in an exercise book grandiose notes intended to shock the indifferent adults on the lawn. It didn't shock them but it liberated him, fantasy his escape route from his father's heavy expectations. He was 15 when his father accused him of not having one single manly pursuit, a remark that burns enduringly through his psyche like hydrochloric acid down the sides of a porcelain bath. He says he longed to be what his father wanted and his brother was, but he was crippled by fear of failure and ridicule. He wagged footy practice. His father's stand-in, the headmaster, required his explanation for this dastardly deed, to be delivered in front of the entire school assembly. Bruce screamed: Because it bores me! He was caned for such insolence and never played the game again until he joined the Royal New Zealand Navy, when he was away from pressure to play. He judged himself a reasonable winger.

His childhood was all about pressure. He spent the summer before secondary school dreading induction. He knew he was a marked lad, as dux of his primary school. He wasn't wrong. While other inductees accepted their dunking, Bruce fought and bit and kicked. He got dunked and then the whole school booed him as a bad sport. That's how we treat swots! one boy yelled at him.

He went on to swot at Victoria University of Wellington, interrupted by service in the army and then navy. In 1945 he returned to complete a BA and marry Diana Shaw, obstetrician. He came back having learned over there fighting for them, that his roots were here. Europe had the best tunes, something to aspire to, from here.

Yet he felt an exile here. He thinks this was because his mother was, a war bride ill at ease in this raw country and telling her children so. He was able to resolve his exile by taking wife and baby to London, where he stayed with

204

theatre friends Edith and Richard Campion. The Masons returned to Tauranga where Bruce managed his in-laws' orchard and wrote, winning the British Drama Festival of one-act plays for *The Bonds of Love*. In 1957 his *The Pohutukawa Tree*, his first play on a Maori theme, was put on by the Campions with the New Zealand Players. While our first professional theatre company did not survive, his play went on to win a huge audience on British television. He got rave reviews there. None of these were mentioned by the New Zealand press, which concentrated on suggesting his play contained racial slurs and the unholy suggestion all was not well back at the pa.

Mason is proud that Maori approved the play and that Inia asked for more. One of the four subsequent Maori plays, *Hongi*, was about a Maori going to Britain and rejecting British culture.

So did Mason in a local context. He had become drama critic on the Wellington morning newspaper *The Dominion* in 1958, keen to use the position to promote local theatre. Two years later he resigned, but this was after a nationally publicised confrontation with visiting theatrical knight Sir Donald Wolfit, who took exception to Mason suggesting his costume as Hamlet was more suited to Falstaff. Wolfit claimed Mason wrote with the rudeness for which New Zealand drama critics were becoming world famous. This might have surprised New Zealanders, who would largely have been unaware of having theatre critics, let alone ones that could be world famous for anything. By the time Mason and Wolfit and many others had had their say in the letters columns, New Zealand theatre had swung on its axis from forelock-tugging to fig off! The *Listener* editorial summed up, suggesting it was now too late for entrepreneurs to see New Zealand as a place where simple inhabitants will welcome third-rate plays and casual productions. Odd really that Sir Donald Bulfit, as he was dubbed by student revueers, was himself a colonial, a Canadian.

Bruce moved the process of decolonialisation forward apace, by provoking ordinary Kiwis. When his play *The Evening Paper* was shown on television in 1965, one letter to Bruce via the editor said, 'I could tear you limb from limb', signed 'New Zealand Mother'. Bruce fondly recalls this was over a play about a Kiwi lad returning here to find people with their heads buried in the sand, only lifting them out to mouth newspaper clichés. More letters accused him of besmirching the name of this fair land, asking God to forgive him his crime against his country, suggesting he was not New Zealand born. His dismissive hand-wave. They were not used to looking in the television mirror.

Mason's mission was to hold up a mirror to purge these defensive problems. He was haunted by a newsreel of Churchill, Stalin, Roosevelt and then Peter Fraser, the local cinema audience exploding with laughter at their leader, as if he was of no account. It meant they thought themselves of no account. Bruce wasn't having a bar of that. We have as much to say, he insists, as the next country.

In over 30 plays Bruce had his Kiwi say. His first 10 years he saw as making no progress, maybe because his plays with 40 characters were too hard to put on in our little theatres. So he did all the characters himself, *The End of the Golden Weather* basically his one-man resolution of this problem. Very Kiwi, very do-it-yourself. The play, or monologue, grew out of radio pieces he had done on his childhood, its theme the Kiwi psychosis that suggests physical performance is the Everest of all human endeavour. His performance pretty well was, playing everybody from child to old man, fat men and thin men, even a middle-aged female not unlike one developing by another male in the Melbourne suburb of Moonee Ponds. For his efforts in June of 1960, the *NZ Herald* critic said Bruce was no Dylan Thomas. He agreed. Nor was he Charles Dickens or Oscar

Wilde, not even Emlyn Williams. He was Bruce Mason, Kiwi.

Audiences knew this. I saw one of his first performances of the piece at Wellington Teacher's College in 1960. We had been laughing at the visiting American satirist Tom Lehrer, and now we were laughing at our own, somebody writing what we recognised as our backyard. Mason nods approval. The shock of recognition, Edmund Wilson calls it. His most satisfying fan was the West Coast mechanic who came backstage to tell him of that recognition.

He did 1500 performances in RSA halls, art galleries, little theatres, sheds, church and school halls, all over the country. Bruce began the dramatic fusion appropriate to our climes. He put the Kiwi into plays. He turned around the Kiwi perception of themselves, made them, allowed them, to accept that their own country was a fit subject for dramatic exposition. This loftily European intellectual got through to West Coast mechanics, making us all laugh and cry at our own childhoods. New Zealand was the prodigal son, Bruce was father who was child unto the Kiwi man. There was a cost. After one performance of *Golden Weather*, someone told him he must have had lovely parents.

Bruce might have happily died laughing, except he said, pulling aside his oxygen mask, he wasn't sure he could ever fully convey the experience of his father transformed into a figure of wild comedy. Diana was in, ushering me out, Bruce with his mask back on, back in his flax bush scribbling new ways to convey the end of the golden weather.

By the same author